MAGISTRATES' COMPANION

MAGISTRATES' COMPANION

by JANET CARTER
LL.B (Hons), Barrister, DPMS, MCIPD

Lawtexts,
PO Box 289,
Leeds LS6 3YG

PUBLISHED FOR JANET CARTER
BY SMITH SETTLE

First published in 2005
for Janet Carter by
Smith Settle
Ilkley Road
Otley
West Yorkshire
LS21 3JP

© Janet Carter 2005

All rights reserved. No part of this book may be reproduced,
stored or introduced into a retrieval system, or transmitted
in any form or by any means (electronic, mechanical,
photocopying, recording or otherwise) without the
prior permission of Smith Settle Ltd and Janet Carter.

The right of Janet Carter to be identified
as the author of this work has been asserted
by her in accordance with the Copyright,
Designs and Patents Act 1988.

ISBN 0-9540636-2-7

British Library Cataloguing-in-Publication data:
A catalogue record for this book is available from the British Library.

Printed and bound by
SMITH SETTLE
Ilkley Road, Otley, West Yorkshire LS21 3JP

Dedicated to my family and friends

CONTENTS

PREFACE xi

Winger competences - element by element

1.	Managing yourself	1
2.	Working as a member of a team	12
3.	Making judicial decisions	17

Chairmanship competence - element by element

4.	Managing judicial decision making	20
5.	**Bail**	
5.1.	General right to unconditional bail	40
5.2.	Statutory exceptions	41
5.3.	Conditional bail	42
5.4.	Custody	45
5.5.	Bail for youths	46
5.6.	Bail application procedure	46
5.7.	Structured approach to bail	47
5.8.	Failure to surrender to bail	48
5.9.	Time limits	49
5.10.	Final points on bail	50
6.	**Case management**	
6.1.	Background	51
6.2.	Case progression officers	51
6.3.	Overriding objective	52
6.4.	Court's case management duties	53
6.5.	Effective case management	57
6.6.	Effective trial management	59
7.	**Procedure and evidence**	
7.1.	Doctrine of precedent	61
7.2.	Criminal and civil cases - differences	62
7.3.	Standard of proof	63
7.4.	Order of proceedings	64
7.5.	The Human Rights Act and its effect	64
7.6.	Types of criminal offences and procedures	68
7.7.	Criminal trial - sequence of events	72
7.8.	Structured approach to verdict	76
7.9.	Search warrants	77
7.10.	Utility warrants	79
7.11.	Basic rules of evidence	79
7.12.	Hearsay	80
7.13.	Bad character	81
7.14	Special measures	84

8.		Sentencing	
8.1. - 8.6.		Structured approach to sentencing and reasons	86
8.7		Sentencing options	93
8.8		Discharge	94
8.9.		Fines and enforcement	95
8.10.		Compensation	104
8.11.		One day detention	105
8.12.		Disqualification	105
8.13. - 8.30.		Community options	106
8.31.		Custody	124
8.32.		Committal for sentence	128
8.33.		Deferred sentence	129
8.34. - 8.44.		Ancillary penalties	130
8.45. - 8.50.		Traffic penalties	137

9.		Role of the legal adviser, pre-court briefing and post-sitting review	
9.1.		Role of legal adviser	145
9.2.		Pre-court briefing	146
9.3.		Post-sitting review	149
9.4.		Effective feedback	151
9.5.		Giving feedback	153
9.6.		Receiving feedback	154

10.	Youth court	
10.1.	Differences between youth court and adult court	156
10.2.	Pre-court interventions	157
10.3.	Role of parent/guardian	158
10.4.	Procedure in youth court	159
10.5.	Remand provisions	163
10.6.	Sentencing options in youth court	166
10.7.	Detention and Training Order	171
10.8.	Structured sentencing for youths	172

COMMON ABBREVIATIONS		176
USEFUL WEBSITES		178
BIBLIOGRAPHY		179
APPENDIX 1 - Sentencing options menu		181
APPENDIX 2 - Fines Calculator		183
INDEX		184

PREFACE

This book provides all aspects of reference for both wingers and chairmen to use alongside the Magistrates New Training Initiative, as published by the Judicial Studies Board. The first four chapters set out the competences and elements with the relevant 'need to know' and 'need to do' information for each.

The most important aspects are cross-referenced for more detailed consideration in the remaining chapters. The implementation of much of the Criminal Justice Act in recent months has created major changes across sentencing, procedure and evidence. Those changes are discussed within the familiar structures, with many examples to clarify the practical effects of the legislation in our daily court lists. The new sentencing options, the consideration of bad character evidence, the implementation of the new case management framework and the impact on bail of a positive drug test are all covered.

In response to feedback on earlier Companions, a full chapter on the youth court has been included. This will serve as a useful refresher for existing panel members and as a comprehensive introduction for new members.

The book may be used as a dip in reference text for specific information, as an update armchair read, or as a self-development aid towards appraisal. It is intended to be a 'one-stop' reference, with all the key features of statute and case law set out as direct quotations as indicated, or by summarising the key points. However, a full bibliography and useful web-site references are given for further reading if required.

Throughout the text I have used the masculine gender purely to avoid tedious repetition to both genders, but please assume the feminine as equally applicable. I have stated the law to the best of my understanding as at the 1st September 2005.

I thank Philip Solity for his help with the traffic and youth sections, the West Yorkshire magistrates and my colleagues for their motivation, and my husband, Neil and our sons John and Andrew, for their patience and support.

Janet Carter
Leeds
September 2005.

CHAPTER 1
COMPETENCE 1
MANAGING YOURSELF

The first four chapters deal with the Adult Court Competence Framework. Chapters 1, 2 and 3 relate to wingers, and chapter 4 to chairmen. The bold print sets out the elements as stated in the Magistrates National Training Initiative (MNTI 2) published by the Judicial Studies Board (December 2003). Discussion of the 'need to know' and 'need to do' of each element is either covered within the chapter or referred to a specific chapter dealing with the subject in more detail.

1.1.1. Before the hearing preparing yourself for your role in the judicial process

1.1.a. Obtaining and reading relevant paperwork prior to the legal adviser briefing and reading all relevant statements and reports as required during the court session.

- Relevant paperwork

The principle reference book in court is the Adult Court Bench Book. This is produced for every magistrate by the Judicial Studies Board and contains:

Section 1: Checklists with a structured approach to all key decisions e.g. bail, sentencing
Section 2: National Mode of Trial Guidelines and Magistrates' Court Sentencing Guidelines
Section 3: Pronouncements
Section 4: Other useful information - Oaths, Naming Systems and 'The Magistrate at Home'.

It is well worth becoming familiar with the lay out of the Bench Book so that reference can be made quickly in court to all relevant aspects.

Examples:

1. Burglary of dwelling - reference materials:

☐ Section 2 - Sentencing Guidelines at p.18 - entry point is given as committal to Crown Court (yellow section for 'criminal' matters)
☐ Mode of Trial Guidelines at p.2.9 - list of factors which would suggest committal to Crown Court, e.g. entry in the daytime when the occupier (or another) is present
☐ Section 3 - Pronouncement at p.37 - committal for sentence.

2. *Driving with excess alcohol - reference materials:*

- Section 2 - Sentencing Guidelines at p.70 - entry point penalty determined by level of alcohol (pink section for traffic cases)
- Section 3 - Pronouncements at p.50 fine, p.54 disqualification, and p.57 attendance on drink driver rehabilitation course
- Reasons for sentence: p.103 of the Sentencing Guidelines (blue section for helpful information). Reasons forms are usually available as separate sheets for reference and completion in court.

Another crucial reference tool is the court register and it is helpful to be fully aware of how to identify all the information it provides, e.g. the nature of any plea entered previously, number of previous listings.

Pre-sentence reports requested by a previous bench are often available before the court begins so that they may be read in advance of the case being called.

1.1.b. Agreeing the roles and responsibilities that you will be undertaking.

The roles which are likely to be delegated are:

- Turning to the relevant page(s) of the Bench Guide Sentencing Guidelines
- Turning to the relevant page(s) of the Bench Guide Pronouncements
- Assessing the net weekly income figure by 'doing the maths' in relation to the relevant fine banding, A, B or C. This is rarely expected to be an exact science, but salaries are usually given in monthly figures and the weekly figure will need to be determined. (See appendix 2 for quick calculator).
- Completing the reasons form as the reasons are agreed.

Some chairmen prefer to undertake particular tasks personally - others will delegate all tasks.

1.1.c. Checking to identify any potential source of conflict of interest in the court business.

1.1.d. Discussion with colleagues and the legal adviser procedural and legal issues including asking about any relevant previous case management decisions.

These elements are covered as specific aspects.
See chapter 7.5.2. Disqualification from sitting.
See chapter 8.2. Pre-court briefing.

1.2. In the court room: conducting yourself effectively in the judicial process

1.2.a. Focussing your attention on what is going on in the courtroom and demonstrating the communication skills required to encourage participation.

- **Listening and non-verbal behaviour**

Listening - the most important skill in court. Particularly in long proceedings, or in 'standard proceedings', listening requires real determination and conscious effort. In court, every word can make a difference to the outcome and everyone who speaks is well aware of this and they are desperately looking to see that the bench are listening. The only way for a speaker to assess that this is happening is to look for the outward signs. They need to be there - attentive eye contact, nodding (not nodding off!), leaning forward, making notes, jotting down a question, and demonstrating that you are referring to it later. Check that the speaker is actually addressing the full bench, rather than selecting the one magistrate (or legal adviser!) who actually looks interested. Looking away from someone who is speaking, or looking down for lengthy periods is tantamount to saying 'not listening - I've already made my decision'.

- **'Make myself listen properly' strategies**

☐ Maintain eye contact with the speaker
☐ Lean forward
☐ Look interested
☐ Nod the information into my head instead of into the mid-air
☐ Look like I am involved in the decision-making
☐ Uncross my arms
☐ Avoid interrupting (write down an aide-memoir word or two for later)
☐ Wait - something good might be coming next ...
☐ Recognise that thought is faster than speech and draw back to what is being said
☐ Formulate a question instead of dismissing 'out of hand'
☐ Do not assume and judge the speaker's motives rather than listening to what they say
☐ Never be in the situation of someone saying to you 'well I said that' and thinking 'did you?'
☐ Acknowledge every contribution from others by doing something with it
☐ Show that I really do agree - say 'yes I agree', 'good idea' (instead of just thinking it)
☐ Show that I am unsure and ask for more information or reasoning - 'why do you think that?' 'what does that mean?'
☐ Check back - 'so you say that ...'
☐ Never think that I always know best.

1.2.b. Taking accurate, succinct notes of relevant issues to assist you and your colleagues in the decision-making process. Asking questions via the chairman in the courtroom to clarify issues and ensure all relevant information is obtained prior to the decision-making.

- **Taking notes**

What is the legal responsibility of a magistrate to take a note? None. The legal adviser does have some specific statutory responsibility to take notes, e.g. of any full argument for bail. Additionally, the Practice Direction 2002 states that:

'At any time, justices are entitled to receive advice to assist them in discharging their responsibilities. If they are in any doubt as to the evidence which has been given, they should seek the aid of their legal adviser, referring to his/her notes as appropriate'.

This carries the inference and expectation that the legal adviser will take some notes in order to perform their responsibilities. However, there are practical advantages for the magistrates to take their own notes.

- Useful to refer and check back in the decision-making process
- Assists in drawing up reasons for a decision
- Assists if the magistrates are asked to state a case for appeal
- Assists an individual to concentrate on the case
- Creates a visual impression of careful interest being taken. Remember to keep looking up and making eye contact to demonstrate that the writing relates to the case, rather than a shopping list!

Avoid trying to take a verbatim note except where key issues are being covered, e.g. statements as to what was said, descriptions. Be ready to alert the chairman to ask witnesses or advocates to slow down.

In the trial scenario there is a school of thought that notes should not be taken during the opening and closing speeches, but only of the actual sworn evidence. This is to emphasise that the magistrates are not considering mere representations as evidence.

Fortunately it is becoming more common for advocates to disclose the basis of the 'not guilty' plea at the pre-trial review and/or at the outset of the case. This alerts the bench to the relevant key issues e.g. mistaken identity, self-defence, and these matters can be noted more fully and underlined for easy reference.

When taking notes it is helpful to split the notes into the structured headings in readiness for the decision making process under the headings. The structures coincidentally flow in the same way as the information is presented. For example, on a guilty plea, the prosecution will focus upon the offence, and predominantly the aggravating features. The defence will focus on offender mitigation. Quotations of remarks made are likely to be significant features of evidence and are worth noting, both on sentence and more particularly, on trial. Questions can be noted as they occur.

Examples:

1. An offence of common assault - guilty plea.

    - Prosecution case - offence (aggravating features)
      Laid in wait outside victim's home at 2am - planned
      'I've got something for you'
      2 blows to the face – clenched fist - black eye

Defendant on bail - trial next month for driving over prescribed limit
Record – assault last year – compensation £250 ordered (Question -
Is it paid?).

- ❑ Defence case - offence (mitigating features)
  Provocation – victim flirting with defendant's girlfriend
  Both parties in drink – both asked to leave club

- ❑ Defence case - offender
  Immediate admission to police – arrested at home at 4am
  Guilty plea today – 1st appearance 5 days after incident
  21 years old – single – full-time work as trainee supermarket manager
  Has signed on voluntarily for 'drink control' course
  (Question - Has he attended yet?)
  Defence suggest conditional discharge!

2. A bail application - offence of theft

- ❑ Prosecution application to remand in custody - exception and reason put forward
  Fail surrender to bail - 2 fail bail convictions in last 12 months

- ❑ Defence application for conditional bail
  Fail surrender - only 2 failures to attend - only fined so mitigation accepted as entry point is community level. Good record of attendance, otherwise, with 8 court appearances in 3 years. Secure address with sister and has a job to start on Monday. (Questions - Have the probation service checked that the sister is content for him to return? Is there any evidence about the job?)
  Defence suggest single condition of residence!

Failure to make notes is not a sign of incompetence. Some magistrates have excellent memories and can contribute effectively on that basis. Most of us simply do not have that facility!

- **Asking questions via the chairman**

Every member of the bench must feel that they have a full picture of the circumstances necessary to make an informed and effective decision. This is a personal judicial responsibility. The example notes above indicate how questions and 'gaps' may be identified as the advocates, defendant and witnesses address the court. When the chairman asks whether there are any questions it is helpful to be ready with succinct wording and if necessary, a clear reason why the information is needed if this is queried.

The general approach about questions from the bench is that the court may ask anything in applications for adjournment and bail, fine default proceedings, exceptional hardship pleas and after conviction with two provisos. Firstly, it must be relevant to the outcome, e.g. enquiries as to whether there was a relationship between the assailant and his victim may lead to imposing a requirement to attend the domestic violence programme. Secondly, it must not amount to making an implication of another offence.

5

For example, 'Did you steal because you are a drug user?' is not an appropriate question. If this information is not volunteered, or revealed from a drug test on charge, then leave this question to the probation service if a report is required.

In trial proceedings, there is a greater restriction. Any questions must simply be as clarification of points already taken. The question in a trial should always be capable of beginning with the expression, 'May we clarify what you said about ....?'. The bench must not enter the arena in a trial, even if there is a glaring question which would surely convict or acquit the defendant! If in doubt, ask the legal adviser who may be able to suggest a re-wording. Questions will often need to be pursued in order to reach and explain sentence. Bear in mind that both the prosecution and defence have their own agendas. The prosecution will emphasise the offence seriousness and their ultimate aim is to obtain a conviction and a sentence to reflect the level of seriousness. The defence will emphasise the offender mitigation, with the aim of achieving a sentence which is palatable to the client. Somewhere in the midst of this, the bench have to look at the balancing exercise from the eyes of the victim and the community. The Press are potentially poised to report the facts which are emphasised the most. This is the report on which the magistracy is likely to be judged by the public. Always imagine the headline of 'Victim's opinion on court decision!' Were sufficient questions raised in open court to understand the victim's standpoint, so that this can be included as appropriate in the reasons and assist in really explaining why the decision was reached.

Example:

> Prosecutor ' *The police have had numerous complaints about disorderly behaviour in this area .....'*

This indicates that there is a problem in the area and the local community will be very interested in the outcome of the case and will be hoping for a strong deterrent penalty. The questions in open court must probe carefully the actual involvement of the defendant on the day and on the offence before the court. He cannot be sentenced for ongoing problems which may have no connection with him whatsoever. The community needs to know the 'full story' about this defendant and the actual evidence against him.

Questions by the bench:

- So far as previous incidents in the area are concerned, is there any evidence that this defendant was involved?
- Do we have a victim personal statement?
- You say that the disturbance began at 9 p.m. - what time did the police become aware of D's presence?
- Please summarise now for us exactly what D actually did and said? (Summary is for the bench and for the public e.g. if there is a protracted and serious incident, is D on the periphery or a ringleader?).

Similarly the bench have the right to take the initiative in pursuing a number of ancillary orders. Questions from the bench will often be necessary to identify whether they are appropriate or not. No one else has such a responsibility. The prosecution will only make suggestions about ancillary orders on a handful of occasions compared to the number of times when they need to be considered by the bench. For instance an application for compensation will usually only be urged if there happens to be a schedule on file. A bolt-on ASBO, usually only if the police have suggested some requirements. The defence solicitor is keen to ensure the minimum interference with his client's liberty. It would be an unusual defence mitigation to introduce the notion of additional penalties, over and above the recommended community order. For instance, a suggestion that in addition to the community order, his client be excluded from licensed premises, pay compensation for terror and distress to the doorman, and be bound over to be of good behaviour in the future!

So who is going to identify whether ancillary penalties are appropriate in the vast majority of cases? The magistrates, and this will often necessitate an important avenue of questioning in order to satisfy three of the five statutory purposes of sentencing - reducing crime, protecting the public and reparation.

1.2.c. Identifying the requirements of court users including those from vulnerable, disadvantaged groups and those with special needs and drawing these to the attention of the chairman if necessary.

1.2.d. Acting at all times with authority and in a dignified and impartial manner.

- The Judicial Oath

This element is largely summarised in the Judicial Oath:

'I ... do swear that I will well and truly serve our Sovereign Lady Queen Elizabeth the Second in the office of the Justice of the Peace, and I will do right to all manner of people after the laws and usages of this realm, without fear or favour, affection or ill will. So help me God.'
An affirmation may be made as an alternative to the oath.
A multi-faith, multicultural, multiracial society makes special demands on magistrates as it poses challenges in court which require an immediate and well-informed response as soon as they arise. In the words of The Lord Chief Justice 'there is a great deal more to understanding the feelings and concerns of ethnic minorities than simply being polite and patient.'

The full range of people in our society across race, religion, culture, sexuality, mental and physical ability, and age appear before the court. Appropriate communication needs to be varied for each individual so that relevant information is given and received in an atmosphere which is comfortable to that individual. This is not just about extending common courtesy.

They may well be dealt with equally but the true test is how the individual perceives the fairness of the court process. The same penalty may well be imposed for the for the same offence, but one defendant was encouraged to give his side of the story and felt that the outcome was fair - the other remained silent and confused in court and left with feelings of resentment.

- **Some basic principles about race, religion and culture**

These are copied directly from 'Race and the Courts' published by the Judicial Studies Board, 1999:

- ☐ Treat everyone who comes to court with dignity and respect - 'do as you would be done by'.
- ☐ Everyone has prejudices. Recognise and guard against your own.
- ☐ Be well informed - being independent and impartial does not mean being isolated from issues which affect people from minority communities.
- ☐ Don't assume that treating everyone in the same way is the same thing as treating everyone fairly.
- ☐ Be 'colour conscious' not 'colour blind'. Fair treatment involves taking account of difference.
- ☐ Don't make assumptions. All white people are not the same, nor are all black, or Asian, or Chinese or Middle Eastern people.
- ☐ Don't project cultural stereotypes. For example that all young black people avoid eye contact as a sign of respect. Most young black and Asian people are second and third generation British born citizens and may be no different from any other teenager when faced with authority figures.
- ☐ Don't perceive people from ethnic minority communities as 'the problem'. The problem may lie in the working methods and traditions of some institutions which may put some groups such as women, people from racial minorities at an unfair disadvantage.
- ☐ If in doubt - ask. A polite and well-intentioned inquiry about how to pronounce a name or about a particular religious belief or a language requirement will not be offensive when prompted by a genuine desire to get it right.

- **Fair treatment - the winger's role**

Whilst it is the chairman who will be speaking directly to parties in court, it is the winger who may well be in a better position to observe potential problems and draw them to the attention of the chairman. Would it be helpful for the carer to actually be alongside the defendant, rather than be sitting at the back of the court? Can the wheelchair user access the relevant part of the court room area easily? If not, where will they be the most comfortable?

Does the date of birth indicate that you have a child or young person before the adult court? If so, a parent or responsible adult should be with them. Is the interpreter struggling to keep up with the prosecutor's outline? Is the interpreter ready to take a break? Should you explore whether a longer lunch break is required on a Friday during a trial involving Muslims (they may wish to attend at the mosque or have some time for prayers)? Did the chairmen check whether the trial date and day of the week was also convenient to the defendant? Can the defendant in custody behind the glass screen actually hear all that is being said by the prosecutor? Was the witness content to take the oath on the bible? Did the defendant feel too intimidated to speak because of the gestures made to him as he came into court by a member of the public?

Whilst the chairman and the legal adviser are naturally focussed on specifics, the winger is in the best position to observe the broader picture in the courtroom, and it may be critical to the perception of fair treatment to alert the chairman. This role can never be underestimated.

1.3. Engaging in ongoing learning and development

1.3.a. Assessing your own performance against the competence framework. Regularly seeking feedback and identifying your learning and development needs on a continuous basis.

1.3.b. Adapting and developing your own performance in the light of changes to law, practice, procedure, research and other developments. Keeping your resource materials (e.g. bench book, handbooks, guidelines) up to date.

One of the cornerstones of the Magistrates New Training Initiative is continuous assessment against the competence framework. Apart from individual consideration, there are also the more formal opportunities.

- **Mentored sittings for new magistrates**

The basis of the six mentored sittings is to use the support of an experienced magistrate in order to transfer the theories of the core training into practical competence in court. The mentor provides support, guidance and advice of a practical rather than technical nature during a short review after each of the six mentored sittings. The review is based on practicalities, reflection on experiences, and clarification, with the expectation that the new magistrate will have questions to ask. The mentor may not be able to deal with every query but will know someone who can!

A record of mentored sittings is maintained throughout the training period. This refers to each of the winger competence elements as an ongoing reference for each review. Sometimes the content of a mentored sitting may provide the relevant experience for the new magistrate to record that they feel competent in a particular element. Sometimes this will be built upon cumulative experiences between sittings. Some mentors may suggest a focus on a particular element between sittings for discussion at the next review.

An interim report is completed by both magistrates between six and nine months of commencing sittings, and a final report at the end of the mentored sittings around the twelve month period, prior to appraisal. The reports ask for identification of any training and development needs and also for the mentor to comment on overall progress. The reports are considered by the Bench Training and Development Committee who may request that suggested topics are emphasised in the twelve hours of consolidation training which is held before the first appraisal. This feedback is very helpful to trainers in order to identify the topics which we evidently did not cover adequately or clearly enough at the core training. Additionally, law and practices can easily change during the twelve months of mentored sittings! Alternatively, other methods of training may offered e.g. directed reading, videos, computer links, one to one sessions, attendance at recommended training events. Everyone is working towards building a competent magistrate, with awareness that every individual will be different and one size and method does not fit all.

- Appraisal

Appraisal is undertaken as a magistrate proceeds to each threshold of a different court role, and at least once every three years thereafter. In the adult court this means that appraisal takes place for the new magistrate after the training period and mentored sittings - between about twelve and eighteen months from beginning to sit in court. If a magistrate wishes to go on to take the chair, then at least two appraisals are required in the adult court before commencing the chairmanship training - one of them within the last three years. This will be followed by at least three and a maximum of six appraisals in the chair, by at least two different appraisers.

If the magistrate chooses to sit in the youth and family proceedings courts, a further appraisal will be required in those courts, first as a winger and then, if appropriate, as a chairman - and then every three years thereafter in the specialist court as well as the adult court. However, youth and adult appraisals may be combined into one appraisal in the youth court until April 2008.

All magistrates are expected to attend six hours of continuation training within the twelve months prior to the three yearly appraisal. A preparation for appraisal checklist is available to identify whether there are any additional training and development needs to be addressed between the training and the appraisal. If they remain unresolved at the time of the appraisal, the appraiser will always ask whether the appraisee has any training requests to be recorded on the appraisal form. Ongoing self-assessment is just as important as the opinion of the appraiser based upon a single court observation and discussion. Whether the request is identified in advance or during the feedback with the appraiser, it is helpful for the appraisee to consider how it will be addressed most effectively for them as an individual. Some of us do not learn well from simply reading - we need to practice and hear feedback. Some of us are not geared to lengthy periods of listening in a large group - we need two-way discussion as a short one to one session on the key points we need to know about. Others may revel in websites and simply need to know where to look, and if there are interactive sites - even better.

The appraisal feedback after court is a two way peer discussion. It is about behaviour which the appraiser has observed in court, and equally, about any other knowledge and behaviour which the appraisee would like to develop within the framework.

- Post-sitting review

This is covered as a specific topic at chapter 9.3. This is an opportunity at every court sitting to review and ask for any assistance or clarification on matters which have arisen during the court. A post-sitting aide-memoir of the competence framework will be available in the retiring room. Any magistrate may use this to make a written request to the Bench Training and Development Committee to deal with any training or development issues which have arisen. Although the process is described as 'post-sitting' review, any points can often be dealt with during any natural break in the court session, and then just check whether there is anything additional at the end of the session. Don't save up for personal appraisal if it can adequately be actioned on the day when it is still fresh in everyone's minds. Many post-sitting review requests are simply about 'We need more information about ...' Very often they can be dealt with for the benefit of the whole bench in the next newsletter.

The post-sitting review also gives the opportunity to give personal feedback on performance - and also to ask for it!

- **Keeping up to date**

Magistrates are presented with a lot of paperwork - bulletins, updates, newsletters, both from the court and from other agencies. A lot more information is also available e.g. internet web sites, The Magistrate magazine for members of the Association, newspaper reports. When the full pages are digested, the reality is often about writing a personal note in the Adult Bench Guide, e.g. Attachment of benefits - increased rate to £5 per week, ASBOs - bolt-on orders may now be made as interim orders. Final summary pages are often worth tearing out and placing at a handy reference point in the Guide. Finally, the legal adviser will highlight relevant major changes at the pre-court briefing. So far as the law is concerned, it is fast-changing to correspond with the changing needs of society. The reassurance is that no one is likely to be completely up to date with every aspect of the law every day. It is a good aim.

CHAPTER 2
COMPETENCE 2
WORKING AS A MEMBER OF THE TEAM

2.1. Making an effective contribution to judicial decision making

2.1.a. Expressing your own views clearly and concisely.

In order to reach a majority or unanimous decision it is important that all views are given clearly so that proper consideration can be given to each contribution. Assertiveness is the key to equal expression and productive outcomes.

Assertive behaviour is about believing that our views are equally as important as anyone else's. Not less important - this results in submissive behaviour. Not more important - this results in aggressive behaviour. We use all three behaviours, but generally it is the assertive behaviour which brings long-lasting positive outcomes and relationships flourish.

Where do the differences lie? Assertive behaviour is about standing up for our own rights in a way that does not violate another person's rights. It is an honest, open and direct expression of a point of view which respects and 'takes on board' other viewpoints.

Submissive behaviour is about failing to stand up for our own rights in such a way that others can easily disregard them. This may be because thoughts, feelings or beliefs are expressed in an apologetic, cautious or self-effacing way or alternatively no clear view or feeling is expressed at all.

Aggressive behaviour is about standing up for our own rights in a way that we violate the rights of another person. Thoughts, feelings and beliefs are expressed in inappropriate ways - often in a patronising, bullying or hostile manner - even though they may very well be the 'right' thoughts! Being more experienced in a particular area can lead to aggressive behaviour because we may well feel that our opinion is therefore more valuable and important. Assertive behaviour is about using our experience to draw people alongside by explaining the salient features. 'Years of experience' are never required for any decision. It is the small, relevant snippets from those years which can usefully be shared.

Assertive statements are usually to the point and we take responsibility by using expressions such as 'I think', 'I believe'. We make clear what is opinion and what is fact, and ask questions to fully understand other viewpoints.

Submissive statements tend to ramble on in an effort to try and justify, and 'I' statements are qualified with expressions such as 'well, it's only my opinion' or 'I don't have much experience of this'. Qualifying words are used such as 'maybe' and filler words such as 'sort of' or 'you know'. Phrases are used which indicate an ease in backing down such as 'it doesn't really matter', or 'well you two are agreed, so I'll leave it there'.

Aggressive statements tend to transfer personal opinion into facts, 'That will never work' rather than 'I don't think it will work'. The views of others are not canvassed or responded to, or they are met with expressions such as 'You cannot be serious'. In a retiring room this cannot be tolerated and the two other members of the bench have to re-establish an assertive discussion. Behaviour breeds behaviour and assertive behaviour is infectious because it makes good sense and will lead to a better outcome.

2.1.b. Questioning the views of colleagues to clarify issues, information, facts and evidence as part of the decision-making process.

Asking questions of one sort or another accounts for at least 25% of most conversations. Formulating questions helps to make us listen and is the best demonstration that we are listening (or not). In the retiring room discussion it is essential to understand exactly what someone else is proposing, and more significantly why they are making that proposal. Getting alongside someone else's thoughts usually needs a few open questions and then some closed questions to clarify the finer detail.

Questions can be used for various purposes in the retiring room.

Examples:

1. To check understanding e.g. 'So you think that a daytime curfew would stop him from shoplifting?'

2. To challenge e.g. 'But surely there are a lot of late night shops in that area?'

3 To seek views e.g. 'What about addressing the underlying drug problem instead?'

Questions can focus more directly on the problem. Statements such as 'I don't understand', is likely to bring forth a mere repetition of what has already been said - perhaps in a louder voice. Asking a question flatters the speaker because it demonstrates both listening and also interest in the viewpoint and allows another opportunity to re-phrase and try to sell an idea.

Questions demand answers, whereas statements can be politely ignored.

2.1.c. Giving equal consideration to your colleagues' contributions including listening attentively and checking your understanding of what has been said.

See chapter 1.2.a. Listening skills in court.

In the retiring room, the listening also involves taking part in the discussion and there is a need for a disciplined approach. A recognition that thought is faster than speech and it is easy to race ahead with our own assumptions, rather than continuing to listen at the speed of the spoken word - someone else's! Assumptions need to be checked out by questions. What exactly does the speaker mean? The worst assumption we can make is that we always 'know best' ourselves - the biggest brick wall of all.

The most important viewpoint may not always be expressed the most eloquently or the most clearly, or indeed, the most loudly. Hear it. Check it out.

2.1.d.   Using appropriate non-discriminatory language. Challenging stereotyping and discriminatory comments made by colleagues.

- Appropriate language and terminology

The list below sets out a number of specific examples of descriptions which may cause offence (X) along with the more acceptable current terminology (✓):

X   Coloured
✓   Black people (Caribbean or African origin), Black British

X   Asian/African if exact origin is known
✓   Asian/African if exact ethnic origin is not known
✓   Region of origin if known e.g. Punjabi, Bengali/ Nigerian, Ghanaian

X   Half-caste
✓   Mixed-race/origin, or dual-heritage

X   Non-white, as it indicates a deviation from the norm
✓   Black, Asian, Chinese etc.

X   Ethnic minority
✓   'Minority ethnic community', makes it clear that the majority is also an 'ethnic' community'.

X   Queer, bent
✓   Homosexual, gay, lesbian

X   Your husband/wife?, if uncertain that they are married
✓   Your partner

X   Wheelchair-bound
✓   Wheelchair-user

X   Handicapped, invalid, cripple, spastic, disabled person
✓   Person with a disability

- Challenging stereotyping and discriminatory comments

It is important to explain that a comment may be perceived as offensive. This may avoid embarrassment for the speaker in the future. Some terms are derogatory, rather than simply 'not politically correct' and may affect the perception of fair treatment and more worryingly, the decision itself - whether today or in the future. Say something, flag it up, or indicate at least by your own body language that such comments and the thoughts that go with them are 'not on'.

See chapter 8.3.c. Giving feedback on sensitive issues.

2.2. Contributing to the working of the team

2.2.a. Building supportive, respectful and constructive relationships with others in the team by adapting your communication style to ensure that you are being understood, minimise interpersonal conflict and demonstrate respect and support to others in the team.

- **Helpful team behaviours**

- Smile
- Use people's names
- When listening, nod and make 'I'm listening' noises such as 'um', 'yes', 'really'
- Summarise back to the other person what you think they have said
- Say things that refer back to what the other person has said
- Show empathy by saying that you understand how the other person feels and can see things from their point of view
- Build on another person's ideas
- When in agreement with another person, openly say so
- Ask open questions
- Be non-judgemental, e.g. by giving personal opinion rather than making statements
- If you disagree, say why. Consider giving the reason first if feelings are running high - this will reduce the chance of interruption
- Admit that there is a conflict of opinion and work to establish the other person's objective before pursuing your own suggestion any further
- Repeat the common ground
- Don't interrupt - jot down the point to come back to
- Identify the difficulties in the alternative view, rather than simply saying 'It won't work'
- Stop and consider whether there is another way forward
- Recognise that anger usually hinders rational thought and behaviour - we can control feelings
- Don't switch off - go into neutral for a few moments and carry on thinking
- Consider whether you are maintaining assertive behaviour or degenerating into aggressive or submissive behaviour (see 2.1.a. above)
- Realise it is 'ok' to say 'I've changed my mind now'
- Bench decisions are based on the majority view - accept the outcome gracefully.

2.2.b. Seeking and being receptive to the advice of the legal adviser.

Discussions with the legal adviser should be solely about law, practice, procedure, penalties and structure and in the main should begin with 'we would like to know' from the chairman, rather than 'I would like to know' from a winger. Identifying the issues for the legal adviser is a team effort.

See chapter 8.1. Role of the legal adviser.

CHAPTER 3
COMPETENCE 3
MAKING JUDICIAL DECISIONS

3.1. Using appropriate processes and structures to facilitate effective decision making

3.1.a. Identifying and agreeing the most appropriate structure for decision making and applying the correct principles to the decision-making structure.

3.1.b. Sifting the relevant information from all that is available and clarifying it when necessary.

3.1.c. Analysing and assessing the information, evidence, facts and submissions within the relevant structure.

3.1.d. Identifying and evaluating the outcomes that flow from the use of the structure and considering any other relevant structure and considering other relevant factors, including the interests of justice.

3.1.e. Assisting in the formulation of reasons and pronouncements.

Structured decision-making is the single most important practical skill in court, and is covered in detail.

See chapter 5.7. Bail.
See chapter 7.8. Verdict.
See chapter 8.1. Sentencing.

3.2. Making impartial decisions

3.2.a. Identifying, acknowledging and setting aside your own prejudices and bias. Including how you might be influenced inappropriately by someone involved in, or an aspect of, the proceedings.

- Prejudice, bias and stereotyping

What is prejudice? The Oxford dictionary definition is 'preconceived opinion, bias (against of or in favour), person or thing' e.g. that a defendant wearing a suit has made a 'one off' mistake but a defendant wearing torn jeans and a 'hoody' is a criminal who was unlucky to be caught this time. Stereotype? An 'unduly fixed mental impression'.

Prejudice is natural. It is part of our daily life and development to build up opinions based on what we see and what we hear - often fleetingly and sometimes without full information or even, completely wrong information! Inevitably there is a danger of that prejudice then moving into an unduly fixed mental impression - a stereotype. This may well go on to influence our thoughts, words and actions in the future.

Once we have a mental picture of someone or something, it is natural to develop assumptions and probabilities around it. This is where we need to recognise the dangers of prejudice and stereotyping and be very clear that whenever decisions are to be made in court, there will never be an element of prejudice or stereotyping entering into the decision. Every defendant, and every case must be dealt with entirely on its own merits. Delete all preconceptions and set the blank screen each time. This may be especially difficult for a magistrate who has recently been robbed, burgled, or been a party to acrimonious family proceedings and it may appropriate to request not to sit on such cases for a short time until emotions have calmed. Subsequently the experience will be valuable - as soon as it is capable of being objective.

Prejudices, stereotypes, labelling, assumptions and generalisations must be recognised. They are natural, but must be left firmly at the court door.

3.2.b. Challenging any bias or prejudice you perceive in the decision-making process.

To 'let remarks go' is to passively collude with discrimination. Very often remarks are made which either demonstrate a generalised view or terms are used which belittle another person without any intention to demean at all. On the other hand, the comment may well be the tip of the iceberg of underlying beliefs and attitudes which could affect decision making and fair treatment today and in the future.

Challenge needs to be made. This may be done through feedback, enquiry or at the least by repeating back the comment and giving the opportunity for it to be withdrawn.

See chapter 8.3.c. Giving feedback on sensitive issues.

3.2.c. Identifying and taking into account factors that are relevant and should legitimately influence a decision; ensuring factors that are irrelevant and that could lead to an unfair decision are not taken into account.

There are numerous examples where there is potential for prejudice to get in the way of dealing with the offence and the individual before the court. Perhaps one of the most obvious situations is dealing with the offence of driving without insurance.

For all who pay their car insurance, it is understandable to feel prejudice against those who drive without having an insurance policy at all. Many of us are paying for the facilities for those who do not pay - that is a fact. The danger is to move into the realms of building prejudiced scenarios and stereotypes around everyone who drives without insurance. This is often based upon facts and figures which have nothing to do with the actual facts of the case.

For instance, the annual premium for someone of the defendant's age would be over £1,000. So what? The actual offence which is proved to the court was committed on a single day of the year and there is no evidence to say that it was ever used before or again. By comparison, a similar remark about 'assuming that he takes cannabis every day then, let's multiply and see how much he would have taken in a year - goodness that must be worth committing to Crown Court!' This would be recognised immediately as being inappropriate in the light of the actual evidence.

'What if' there had been an accident and the victim would have no recompense? But there was no accident or charge of careless driving. 'What if' thoughts and comments have no place in decision-making. By comparison, a similar remark on a criminal damage case on the lines of 'what if someone had been stood near the window when it was broken?' would be recognised immediately as being inappropriate in the light of the actual evidence.

The uninsured driver often touches a non-judicial nerve because prejudice is natural, especially when we are affected directly by increased premiums. On the whole, most of us have no reason at all to be particularly prejudiced against cannabis users and those who cause criminal damage and it is so much easier for us to recognise where the lines have to be drawn wearing a judicial hat. It is much easier to focus on this case, this defendant and these facts. Prejudice is not wrong, it is natural. It simply has to be recognised and left at the court door.

CHAPTER 4
COMPETENCE 4
MANAGING JUDICIAL DECISION MAKING

The bold print sets out the elements of the chairmanship competence as stated in the Magistrates National Training Initiative (MNTI 2) published by the Judicial Studies Board (December 2003). Discussion of the 'need to know' and 'need to do' of each element is either covered within the chapter or referred to a specific chapter dealing with the subject in more detail. The chairmanship competence falls into 4 headings:

4.1. Relationship with the legal adviser
4.2. Managing the court proceedings
4.3. Managing the decision-making process
4.4. Self development.

4.1. **Relationship with the legal adviser**

4.1. **As the chairman working in partnership with colleagues and the legal adviser to ensure the effectiveness of the court.**

4.1.a. Identifying issues for clarification prior to each court session and establishing the relevant structures and processes to facilitate routine applications and procedures.

4.1.b. Agreeing with the legal adviser respective roles and responsibilities and maintaining these

4.1.c. Reviewing the day's sitting with the legal adviser.

The role of the legal adviser, pre-court briefing and post-sitting review are considered in detail as specific topics at chapter 9.

4.2. **Managing the court proceedings**

4.2 **As the chairman managing court proceedings using appropriate communication skills.**

4.2.a. Ensuring that the purpose and framework of the hearing is established and maintained from the outset by giving appropriate directions, setting realistic timetables, seeking explanations from participants for failure to comply with directions and taking appropriate action.

- **Case management**

Since the implementation of the Criminal Case Management Framework in April 2005, case management is now one of the major features of chairmanship and chapter 6 covers this in detail.

- **Using questioning techniques to gather information**

The most effective tool of case management is an ability to adopt an inquisitorial approach to any application for adjournment. This means questions - any questions which will inform the bench sufficiently to make a fair decision for both sides. Basically there are no limits provided that the question can be justified as being relevant. Just as the advocates can choose the information they will give voluntarily, the bench may choose the information which they believe they need. This isn't a trial when questions are restricted to those which clarify the information chosen by the advocates, which is often frustrating. There are no such limits with adjournment applications.

It is important to recognise that all three magistrates are on the information trail, albeit the questions will normally be asked by the chairman. The reality is that the chairman will often be absorbed with the defendant and advocates, and it is the wingers who will have the greater facility to observe, and process the information and be the 'eyes and ears' of the bench. The most important question in most cases is the genuine question to each winger, 'do you have any questions?' - is there anything else the bench needs to know to make a fully informed decision? Questions obtain information but they also show that the court is interested, listening attentively and managing effectively.

- **Questioning - questions relating to case management**

These questions use an inquisitorial approach, i.e. any relevant questions can and should be asked in determining the issue of whether or not to adjourn a case.

Question type	Purpose	Example	Suggested use
Closed	Aim is to get a 'yes' or 'no'	Was the court made aware at the pre-trial review that this witness was to be called?	Obtains the information in stark terms, but further questions may be necessary
Open	Cannot be answered by a 'yes' or 'no'.	Why is the witness not here today?	Forces the need to give clear explanation.

| Probing | Follow-up for more | Why can't the witness be contacted today? | Funnelling down from broad statements into critical information. |
| Hypothetical | 'What-ifs' to assess possibilities | What if we heard the prosecution case today?

We are considering an order for wasted costs as the adjournment appears to be based on your omission to warn your witness. What are your comments on whether this order would be appropriate? | Enables various options or potential decisions to be explored fully. |

4.2.b. Giving clear instructions to participants throughout the proceedings and checking that all those involved understand what is happening in the courtroom and any decisions that have been made.

- **Opening the court proceedings**

Although courts may have slightly different local practices, the most common starting point is that the bench will enter court at the court starting time, whether or not there is any business to proceed with. This demonstrates that the court is ready to proceed and enables the chairman to establish early authority, greet those present and openly make such enquiries as:

☐ Is there anything we can proceed with e.g. paperwork, assisting other courts?
☐ Who is bailed to attend at 10 a.m.?
☐ Have they attended? If not, this can be taken up with them when they do attend.
☐ Which solicitors are we waiting for? Do we know where they are? In practical terms it is impossible for solicitors to be in two courts at once, but as a matter of courtesy and list juggling it is critical that they keep in touch with the court as to their whereabouts and expected time of arrival.

In liaison with the legal adviser it may then be possible to assess a time for the bench to return so that everyone is aware that there is a real expectation of making a start at a specific time and at least re-assessing the difficulties. Alternatively, the bench may prefer to await notification that the list is ready to proceed.

- **The 'running commentary' during the proceedings**

It is helpful if the chairman effectively gives a running commentary of exactly what is happening. This is simply about making sure that everyone in court - defendant, usher, dock officer, probation officer, and the general public know exactly what is happening and what is required of them. Open justice is visible and audible. Management from the chair is far preferable to unexplained whisperings which can seriously distract the proceedings and leave people confused about what is going on.

Examples:

1. *Defendant pleads 'Not Guilty'. He remains standing. All is quiet except for the legal adviser making a prolonged whispered telephone call to someone. Who? The witnesses? The police? Are they coming today? Is the trial going to happen today or not?*

So much better if the chairman says 'We are going to fix a date for the trial and the legal adviser is going to obtain some dates so that we can fix a date that is convenient to you and all the witnesses. This may take a few moments - do sit down'. This also takes the pressure off the legal adviser who is probably ringing a number which is engaged for several minutes!

2. *A case is proceeding. The court probation officer returns to court to conduct a stand down enquiry on the previous case. He asks the usher to identify the defendant, then has a conversation with the legal adviser to ascertain the basis of the report required, then interrupts the prosecutor to obtain the file and then tells the waiting defence solicitor how long he will take. Meanwhile another advocate is attempting to mitigate effectively in the current case. The bench is distracted by the inevitable noise and movement.*

So much better if the chairman finds a place to pause and says ' Mr. Advocate could I just interject briefly so that we can give you our full attention. Mr. Probation we have stood down the case of Mr. Defendant (point to him) to consider unpaid work at the low level. Mr. CPS do you have the file for the probation officer? Thank you. Now, Mr. Advocate you were saying ....'

- **Addressing special needs**

Special needs may well be identified before or during the court sitting. This is an important area of expertise as the court must be able to accommodate the special needs of defendants and witnesses to ensure that they have, and also perceive that they have a fair hearing.

'Equal treatment - do's and don'ts'. These are summarised from the Judicial Studies Board publication 'Equality before the Courts' (2001):
Do:

☐ Recognise that Christians have 'Christian' names - others do not.
☐ Ascertain how parties wish to be addressed.

- Obtain details of any disabilities or medical problems of the parties and allow more time for special arrangements, e.g. seating, breaks on request.
- Plan in advance for disabled people so that their needs are accommodated, e.g. space to move a wheelchair with ease.
- Ensure that appropriate measures are taken to protect vulnerable witnesses. Children should always be accompanied by a parent or responsible adult in court, and should normally be referred to by their first name. Child victims of violence and sexual offences will normally give their evidence via video link. This extends to vulnerable and intimidated adults in October 2005.

Don't:

- Underestimate the stress of appearing in court, particularly when the ordeal is compounded by an additional problem such as disability or appearing without professional representation.
- Overlook the use - unconscious or otherwise - of gender-based, racist, religious or homophobic stereotyping as an evidential short-cut.
- Allow advocates to attempt over-rigorous cross-examination of children or other vulnerable witnesses.
- Allow anyone to be put in a position where they face hostility or ridicule.

In dealing with people with a disability there is various guidance which includes the following key points:

- Check whether the carer should accompany at all times - even in the dock or witness box.
- Ensure that waiting time is kept to an absolute minimum.
- Talk directly to the person with the disability. This includes those with a learning disability. It is tempting to speak instead to the person accompanying them as they will very often be making the responses on behalf of the person.
- When talking to a person with a hearing difficulty, make sure that your face is in the light, look at them directly and speak clearly and naturally in a strong volume which you can maintain. Keep your hands away from your mouth. Ask them if you are speaking loud enough rather than shouting at the outset.
- A person who is deaf and without speech is a competent witness if he can understand the nature of an oath. This may be established either by signs, through an interpreter or in writing. The evidence must be expressed sufficiently clearly to enable it to be faithfully interpreted.
- When talking to a blind person, introduce who you are and ask each speaker to introduce themselves before beginning their speech so that the person can orientate himself first.
- Ask if a person needs any help, but wait until it is accepted before doing anything.
- A wheelchair is part of the body space of the person using it and nobody in the court should simply move it without permission.
- Consider whether more food or drink is required. Provide opportunities to take medication and arrange for easy request for toilet breaks.
- When there is a language difficulty, the court must provide the free assistance of an interpreter if the defendant cannot understand or speak

English. This is not means related and is an obligation under Article 6 of the Human Rights Act. The court holds a list of approved interpreters and fees are payable to the interpreter. It is important to speak slowly, allow plenty of time for interpretation and in a lengthy trial, allow relaxation breaks for the interpreter.

In general terms for all defendants and witnesses, it is important to make sure that they can hear easily and have the confidence to let the chairman know if they cannot. This applies particularly to defendants who appear in custody behind a glass screen, with the advocates angled away from the dock and towards the bench.

4.2.c. Addressing those in court fluently, clearly and audibly at all times

- **Content of the pronouncement**

Model pronouncements are produced in section 3 of the Adult Court Bench Book. The aim is to cover all essential elements in straightforward, jargon-free, plain language. It is accepted that chairmen may well modify the language and adapt to their own style and to the particular individual they are speaking to. New chairmen may find it helpful to work through the regular pronouncements and put in words and phrases which they are more comfortable with, and then check out with a legal adviser. Similarly it is worth marking in the points where there will be a pause, either to cross-refer to another pronouncement, or to check understanding. There is no problem about 'not referring to the book' but this is likely to need practice and the discipline to ensure that you are constantly up to date with the modifications needed.

As a basic requirement, virtually every pronouncement will need to cover:

- ❏ Detail of the decision - What is it and how much/how long is it?
- ❏ Explanation - What needs to be done?
- ❏ Warning(s) - What will happen otherwise?
- ❏ Reasons - Why is this decision being made?

The basic reference material for a pronouncement could well involve the completed reasons form; the basic community order; the specific requirements, and the compensation pronouncement - potentially five pieces of paper to move smoothly through....

- **Effective delivery of the pronouncement**

So far as effective delivery is concerned, the key points are:

- ❏ Engagement with the individual concerned. Personalising by using the defendant's name at the start, end, and in the middle of a long pronouncement. Body language and eye contact which says 'you are important and this is between you and me - adult to adult'. 55% of the communication is going to be based on what the individual can see, rather than hear.
- ❏ Simple language and no descriptions which use jargon, e.g. 'You are a 'totter'', and no acronyms e.g. 'attend a 'DIDs' programme.'

- Volume which is loud enough for everyone in court to hear easily and effortlessly. For those who are normally quietly spoken, it may need a deliberate effort to take in plenty of breath to provide the fuel and then throw the words like tennis balls on to the far wall. New chairmen may need to find and practice their 'pronouncement' voice.
- Pace which is steady enough for the defendant to catch all that is said, especially towards the end of a lengthy pronouncement. Feeling 'slow' is probably about the right pace.
- Pauses which allow time for the defendant to digest each piece of information before moving on to the next part. Some time is needed for the internal dialogue, e.g. 'So, I'm not going to prison!' before moving on to the next 'bit' e.g. 'So, how long will I be doing unpaid work for?' It is helpful to regard the change from one aspect of the decision to another, often involving changes of page in the Bench Book, as a helpful pause for the defendant rather than as a panicky silence for the chairman.
- Tone and pitch which has some variation between the explanation and the warning elements. This will flag up that there are important implications to be understood even after the decision itself is given. The amount of the fine is likely to be of the most interest, but the warning that non-payment can result in custody is the most important.
- Checking understanding by responses through eye contact and body language, and a verbal check. Simply asking 'Do you understand?' is almost certainly going to bring the reply of 'yes', given the occasion and the environment. It may occasionally be helpful to ask the defendant to repeat back, e.g. complicated bail conditions, when you feel that the bail notice is unlikely to be read after court. This might be done on the lines of 'Can I just check with you that I've covered the detail clearly enough?' rather than, 'And now, repeat back to me'.

Particularly in long pronouncements there is much to be said for following the trainers' strategy of repetition:

- 'Tell them what you're going to tell them' - 'The sentence will be a fine, disqualification and costs'.
- 'Tell them' - give the details of each aspect.
- 'Tell them what you've told them' - 'So the total due is ... and the disqualification is for ...'

Sometimes there are implications for others. Does the probation officer understand which options or issues should be covered in the report? Does the victim understand that the compensation will be paid in instalments when paid by the defendant rather than by a lump sum? Does the dock officer understand that the one day detention is deemed to have been served? Does the press officer understand that reporting restrictions apply?

Relying upon a written notice of decision to the defendant is insufficient on its own. Many defendants cannot read – even more, do not.

4.2.d. Encouraging participants at the hearing to contribute constructively and dealing assertively with any inappropriate, inaccurate or unhelpful contributions by restricting representations, speeches and discussions and dealing promptly with any behaviour that is or may disrupt the functioning of the court.

- Encouraging contributions from unrepresented defendants

Assume that the legal adviser has identified the defendant and dealt with the formalities of identification, advance disclosure, charge/plea. The defendant does not wish to take advantage of legal representation or advice and the legal adviser then asks the chairman whether the defendant may be seated, i.e. he has completed his part. What next?

Most defendants desperately want 'to do the right thing at the right time' in court. The court can ensure that at least that concern is allayed and leave the defendant free to consider the crucial aspect of what he needs to say to the court.

If the agreement is for the chairman to take control, a suggested process is described below, which should ensure that both sides of the case are presented in as much detail as if a defence solicitor had been instructed.

- Explanation of procedure to an unrepresented defendant

A brief commentary is essential so that the defendant is able to fully understand who is who, and what is happening at each stage of the proceedings, and contribute effectively to a fair hearing.

Example:

'Mr. X, you may be seated now. The prosecutor for the Crown Prosecution Service (show whom you mean) will give the court an outline of the prosecution version of what happened. Listen carefully. Then you will have the same opportunity to tell us your version of what happened.

An important factor is to use the same words for each input e.g. 'version of what happened'. It does not create an even-handed appearance if the prosecution input is described as 'the prosecution facts' and the defendant's response is encouraged by the words 'and then we will hear your story'!

A comment such as 'same opportunity' as above, helps to underline parity, and also the expectation of similar 'air-time'.

It may be appropriate to offer notepaper and a pen, but this should be considered with some care, particularly on a guilty plea. The legal adviser will have checked that any initial disclosure has been served. It may even be in the hands of the defendant at the time, and this should provide a satisfactory summary of what is to be said. It may be necessary to check that the defendant has actually had time to read the disclosure and has been able to do so. Any inference that note-taking is expected may create a feeling of disadvantage if it is not taken up for any reason. In unfamiliar circumstances note taking is a challenge for most people. The chairman and/or wingers should ensure that the bench takes notes so that particular points can be pursued as appropriate.

- **Gathering information and encouraging mitigation by questioning**

Ideally this should begin with some open questions which may be successful in obtaining information. It may assist to begin by setting the scene and demonstrating that the court is listening, fully engaged and is genuinely alongside the defendant in their mitigation.

Examples:

1. *'Now, Mr. X, we would like to hear your version of what happened. What did happen?'*
2. *'So Mrs. Y, it's last Monday morning at 10 a.m. and you are in XXX store. Please talk us slowly through exactly what happened'.*
3. *'What was happening in the pub just before the police arrived?'... 'And what were you doing?' ...'And then?'... 'Why did you do that?'*

The 'big avoid' - Would you like to tell us what happened? This is a closed question and the answer may well be 'no'. Compounded by a second closed question, 'Are you sure?'!

- **Questioning - examples relating to an unrepresented defendant**

Question type	Purpose	Example	Suggested use
Open	Cannot be answered by a 'yes' or 'no'	What happened? Why did you do that? What do you pay out each week?	Start up of any interaction with an unrepresented defendant and in the retiring room.
Closed	Aim is to get a 'yes' or 'no'	Are you sure that you will start work on Monday? Will you pay as ordered this time? Do you understand that you could go to prison if you don't comply with the order?	'Need to know' critical features of decision-making. Flags up in simple terms stark realities. Asking and checking is always more effective to get messages across, than simply 'telling'.
Reflect-ive	Mirrors back to encourage more	So you say that you were not thinking straight at the time ... and why was that ...?	A listening/caring approach is likely to draw out helpful information.

Probing	Follow-up for more	Did you take out the bank loan after the fine was imposed?	Funnelling down from broad statements into critical information.
Hypothetical	'What-ifs' to assess possibilities	What problems might you have if you were excluded from going into X street?	Where there is a range of possible outcomes which depend upon a range of scenarios.
Leading	Based on expected or anticipated answer	So you have had the money to pay the fine?	Challenges the defendent with the bench's understanding of the facts.
Multiples	Several questions rolled into one	Will you tell us about the incident and exactly what time it happened and what you saw?	Always pause after the first question for a response and avoid multiple interrogations.

Example: A plea of exceptional hardship to avoid a points disqualification
- What is your employment? *(Open)*
- You say that you need a licence to do your job, tell us more about what your job involves?*(Reflective)*
- How many times each week do you have to deliver cars? *(Closed)*
- Is this actually part of your job description?*(Probing)*
- Would it be possible for someone else to do the deliveries? *(Hypothetical)*

Keep the questions short. Explain, if necessary, why you need to know. The defendant may well misinterpret what or why you are asking and may be unnecessarily wary of giving the answer. Be ready to re-phrase if there is no helpful response.

Example: A means enquiry

'Who lives with you?' X

No response. The defendant may not wish to supply names or relationships in open court and, perhaps understandably, does not see what this really has to do with the case before the court. Explain the context.

'We need to have a picture of your financial situation so that we can fix a fair fine. Do you have any dependants to support out of your income? Does anyone else contribute to the rent?' ✓

- **Encouragement to the defendant who is not engaging**

Some further explanation may be necessary to deal with concerns such as 'dropping myself in it even more' and 'least said - best mended'. The message heard at the time of charge is likely to be on the lines of 'anything you do say, may be taken down and used in evidence against you' and this may well play on minds at the time of the court hearing as well.

Examples:

1. *'Mr. X, it's important for us to fully understand exactly what happened so that we can fix the most appropriate penalty for you. To do that, we need to hear both sides of this incident.'*

2. *'Mr. Y, we must disqualify you for at least 6 months because you have 12 penalty points now, <u>unless</u> you can convince us that you will suffer exceptional hardship, that is, that you will face problems which would be worse than normal for a disqualified driver. Before we sentence you, we need to know if you would have any serious difficulties without a licence.'*

It is important to jot down any factors which are likely to aggravate seriousness, so that they can be raised as questions with the defendant. An opportunity must be given for a response, before they appear as facts in the reasons.

Example:

Chairman: *'Mr. X, the police officer says that he told you to go home three times and you deliberately ignored him - what can you tell us about that?'*

Defendant: *'I was just so drunk I can't remember him asking me to do anything. If I'd been sober, I'd have gone straightaway. I just wish I had.'*

The response may well satisfy the bench that this was not a deliberate lack of co-operation as it may at first appear, and that there is some remorse about the situation. Alternatively, the officer may not have been in uniform, may have been aggressive, or the defendant was frightened to leave the scene and walk home alone in fear of a further attack. The safest assumption is that there is another version to the facts, rather than that the prosecution facts give an all-encompassing picture.

- **Relevant questions?**

Consider whether a question is really necessary and relevant. Is it really going to affect the decision and the way it is implemented?

Examples:

1. In fixing a fine:
   Are you married? Does the children's father live with you?

What do the personal relationships of the household matter? The only issue is how many people live on the income described and in a public court, any further detail is unnecessary in order to fix the amount of a money order.

2. *In enforcing a fine:*
   How much is spent on beer/cigarettes/lottery/DVD player/Sky TV?

Some people's luxuries are the necessities of others. We all have some awareness of how much is needed for day to day life and that amount should be protected - even though choices as to how a limited budget is spent will vary. Smoking may well be a chosen necessity and it is the family food bill which will most likely take the brunt of a high instalment rate, rather than a reduction in cigarettes.

- **Dealing with disruptive and discourteous behaviour**

All advice tends towards taking a soft approach initially. Creating respect by first giving respect. It may avoid the degeneration into a teacher/child interchange which is so easily triggered by immediate confrontation. Demonstrating the equality of a reasonable adult to adult relationship will enable the potentially nervous defendant to confidently go on to give his mitigation, and the angry member of the public to feel that justice will be done. The polite instruction may be all that is necessary.

Examples:

1. To the member of the public who has made loud comment:
   'You are welcome to stay in court and listen, provided that there are no more interruptions. Otherwise we will have to ask you to leave so that we can concentrate on the evidence being given.'
2. To the defendant with his hands in his pockets who is not making eye contact:
   Explain the procedure as with any other defendant. Once he has had the opportunity to settle down, then decide whether he is being deliberately discourteous or is simply unsure how to behave in court.
3. To the defendant who protests loudly as he is taken to custody:
   'Please go with the officer'. Consider whether the defendant's emotional remark is really worth calling a defendant back to court at this stage. He is going to custody in any event and the proceedings have finished. A measure of 'not hearing' such remarks may be the more dignified option, rather than inciting further comments and potential contempt proceedings.

If the dignity of the court is not restored, then the next suggested stage is to give a clear warning of the contempt powers. Then retire briefly for reflection and for composure to be restored - and also for an officer to be located for escort to the cells if this becomes necessary.

- **Contempt of court**

This occurs if a person wilfully insults a magistrate, any witness, officer or advocate either during the court or in going to or returning from the court, or if a person wilfully interrupts the proceedings of the court, or wilfully misbehaves in court.

The court sanctions are to order the offender to be taken into custody and detained until the court rises, and in addition, if appropriate, a penalty of imprisonment up to 1 month or a fine up to £2,500. The court may discharge the committal at any time. Note that there is no power to commit a youth for contempt.

If the defendant is removed, he must be warned of the actual contempt powers and be offered legal representation. At any stage he may be returned back to the court to apologise and this will normally mark the end of the incident. In theory, the case could be dealt with in the absence of the defendant but it is preferable to simply stand the case down for a 'cooling off' period, and hope for an apology to be forthcoming.

If formal contempt proceedings and punishment are necessary, this will normally be dealt with at the end of the court list by admission or denial. The defendant may object to being dealt with by the same bench. A denial should always be dealt with by a different bench. This should be as soon as possible, with the consideration of bail in the meantime. The opportunity to apologise should be on offer at all times. Custodial sentences should only be imposed where there really is no practical alternative.

- **Ensuring that witnesses are not bullied**

There is a fine line between robust cross-examination, which is allowed to test out the veracity of the witness, and bullying which is using verbal power to coerce others by fear. The line must not be crossed. When answers are drawn out in a hostile environment, they may be motivated simply by wanting the questions to stop and to get out of the room. The chairman may consider various interventions.

Examples:

1. Summarise what the witness has answered e.g. 'Mr. Y has now said three times that he cannot remember the colour of the car - may we move on now?'

2. Ask where the line of questioning is leading if it is becoming protracted and unclear. At the least it should focus the mind of the questioner.

3. Suggest that the witness may need a short break and the bench will retire after a particularly lengthy or emotional line of questioning.

4. Cut off allegations of lying, concocting or 'making up stories' with a statement from the chairman that they are matters for the court to determine after hearing all of the evidence.

- Dealing with discourteous advocates

How should the chairman deal with advocates who begin a whispered conversation in court whilst waiting for their case to be called? This can be very distracting for those involved in the present case, and of course the bench. A comment that the bench is finding it difficult to concentrate because of the noise, might also carry the suggestion that they conduct their conversation outside of the court, with the assurance that the usher will call them into court as soon as their client's case is called.

There is also the situation of the advocate who has kept the court waiting. It is important to recognise that the client in court wishes to feel that he is being well represented and that his choice of advocate is respected by the court. The discourtesy of arriving late can be dealt with more fully and more sensitively after the client has left the court. If the explanation is unsatisfactory, the matter may be reported to the Clerk to the Justices. He may pursue this by reporting the incident to the Law Society and/or Legal Services Commission, particularly if a pattern of behaviour is emerging.

Ignoring late arrivals or negative behaviour is to the detriment of defendants and witnesses and encourages similar repetitions. When a confidential explanation is sought afterwards, and it is reasonable, the incident is then closed on a positive note for the solicitor and the chairman and will avoid future tension.

4.3. Managing the decision-making process

4.3 Seeking and enhancing the contribution of colleagues in order to ensure effective decision-making.

4.3.a. Asking colleagues to take responsibility for key tasks.

4.3.b. Facilitating discussion by focusing on the structure, identifying and summarising key issues, intervening promptly when disagreement is preventing constructive discussion and progressing and exploring areas of disagreement in order to achieve a resolution.

4.3.c. Agreeing the decision, reasons and pronouncement to be given in court.

4.3.d. Reviewing the day's sitting with your magistrate colleagues and/or the legal adviser and seeking, receiving and giving feedback.

See:
Chapter 9. Pre-court briefing and post-sitting review.
Chapter 5.7. Structured decision-making on bail.
Chapter 8.1. Structured sentence.

- **Getting the discussion started and summarising key issues**

It is relatively easy for two people to have a conversation. It is quite a different matter to manage a discussion between three people and reach a conclusion. There is the ever present danger of moving from three way discussion to two way conversation with an observer present. That person might be the new magistrate, the only man with two women, the only one who did not watch a particular television programme the night before, or the only one who does not follow football. Even before court, there is a team to build in readiness for decision making later in the day and encouraging full participation of all three members.

Once in the retiring room, the first stage is to ensure that everyone is referring to the relevant reference material and ready to work through the appropriate structured approach, following a short introductory summary by the chairman.

Examples:

1. *Sentencing on a common assault case*

- *What is required?*
  Sentencing Guidelines: Common assault
  Structured reasons form
  Notes.

- *Opening outline:*

  . *'The Guideline entry point for common assault is a community penalty. So let's look at the offence itself first. Mrs. X, would you like to start off with your views on any aggravating features ....'*

The chairman needs to make it clear that he is not going to entertain any discussion about whether colleagues are 'for or against the report recommendation' or take any views at all on options until the case has been discussed. The last words in court will have come from the defence about options and it is essential to re-wind back to the prosecution outline first and work through the structure - Offence, Offender, Objectives and Options. See 8.1.

2. *Trial of a common assault case*

- *What is required?*
  Structured reasons form for verdict
  Notes
  (NOT the Guidelines at this stage!).

- *Opening outline:*

  'So just to summarise what we have been told in court on the law. The prosecution must prove beyond reasonable doubt that the defendant put the victim in fear of immediate unlawful violence at the least. Is that your understanding?'

'I suggest that the agreed facts are that there was an argument between the two of them and at some stage the defendant did strike the victim in the face with a single blow and cause a black eye. Do we agree that?'

'The disputed fact is that the defendant says that he struck the blow in self-defence because he really believed that the victim was going to strike him first. The victim says that nothing was said or done to suggest there would be any violence at all. That is the issue and we need to look carefully at the evidence to assess whose evidence we prefer. Do we agree that it is the issue of the self-defence that we need to focus on?'
'Mrs. Y, what is your view of Mr. Z's evidence? ....'

This approach will avoid a general discussion which re-iterates again and again what is either agreed or irrelevant. This is particularly easy to fall into if the method of discussion is to go through every line of every witness. After hearing both sides, much of what is said is actually agreed and the 'padding' can be ignored.

By reminding colleagues of the 'beyond reasonable doubt', it can reduce lengthy 'what if/maybe/not sure' meandering. The chairman who quickly focuses and checks out the disputed points for careful analysis will save time and reach a high quality, well-reasoned decision. A clear verdict structure. What is to be proved? What is agreed? What is disputed? Preferred evidence and why? See 7.8.

3. Bail decision

- What is required?
  Structured reasons/bail form
  Pronouncements - Conditional bail/Remand in custody
  Notes.

- Opening outline:

  'The prosecution application is to remand in custody based on the exception of failure to surrender because of the two previous failures, and the defence have listed a number of conditions for us to consider'

  'The starting point is unconditional bail. 'Do we agree with the one exception to unconditional bail for that reason?'
  'Do any other exceptions or reasons apply?'
  Now, let us consider whether any conditions would satisfy us?'

A bail discussion has the highest potential to begin with the echoes of the defence submission, 'Well I'd be happy with those conditions'. A competent chairman will discourage 'rubber-stamping' and ensure that the only discussion about conditions will follow on from the exceptions (grounds/risks) which the bench have agreed. See 5.7.

- **Managing disagreement and potential conflict**

Disagreement is going to happen and it must be managed so that everyone feels that they have had their say and everyone has listened effectively. So

35

long as this happens, disagreement can have constructive consequences and is 'ok'. It can increase motivation, innovative thinking and generate a thorough examination of the alternatives.

Conflict arises from various classic conditions and in the retiring room it is usual to find that there are different preferred outcomes. This conflict can be avoided by making sure that outcomes are left right to the end of a structured approach so that the relevant information is identified and agreed first on a stage by stage basis.

In a sentencing case, the early establishment of the level of seriousness will narrow down the outcome to one band or another e.g. community band. The next stage is to identify the sentencing purpose(s) to be achieved. This is often omitted and the discussion of options suffers from a lack of common purpose. If it is agreed that there is realistic hope for rehabilitation or a need for straight punishment, then the outcomes and potential for conflict are necessarily reduced at the next stage. Similarly, it may equally arise that all agree that some prevention is also required, and preventative 'add on' penalties will then fall to be discussed, but a reduced and specific menu is at least agreed. Co-operation and mutual respect is more likely to be generated on the back of some level of agreement and progress together.

Similarly, in bail and verdict cases, there are matters which are likely to be agreed first. Enjoy them. Then be sure to narrow the issue as much as possible before even mentioning final outcome. Initial views may be changing or developing in the meantime and the potential conflict may have ebbed away. If we move forward carefully, we seldom have to go backwards. Going back over old ground, and re-visiting omissions creates unhelpful feelings of irritation and frustration, the more so because it can be avoided.

Some tools for managing conflict are:

- Make sure that the visual aids are being used - structured approach, guidelines and reasons form.

- Make statements about what is agreed.

    'We agree that the offence seriousness falls within the community band.'
    'We agree that the record shows that some rehabilitative option is needed here.'
    'We agree that he is likely to commit offences on bail.'

- Question everything else.

- Never tell two people to stop arguing - they probably will not. If they do, the quietness will be uncomfortable. Make them pause instead by asking a question. A straight 'why?' can sound accusing - soften it with a positive if possible.

    'So we have a difference of view to share. Mrs. X, you suggest a curfew requirement and that is in the community band as we agreed. Why do you think it is the most effective choice?'

- Repeat back the argument of each winger to focus and check understanding.

    'So Mrs. X you say ... because ... '
    'Is there anything else you would add to support your view?'
    'And Mr. Y you say ... because ...'
    'Is there any anything else you would add to support your view?'

- Check out that those in conflict are actually listening and understanding each other's view point rather than concentrating on pursuing their own view.

    'Can you see where Mrs. X is coming from?'
    ' Why do you disagree with it?'

- Identify where the specific facts of the case are distorting into broad emotion or bias.

    'I can understand that cases of domestic violence are abhorrent to you. I'm also aware of the high likelihood of previous history, but we have no evidence of any history in this case, do we?'

- Suggest alternatives as an equal member of the team, rather than as a chairman who is trying to compromise.

    'I don't believe that the criteria are made out for us to add an Anti Social Behaviour Order in this case. But I do think the facts of the case call for some measure of protection for the future. A short specific bind over would be proportionate and it may help to prevent a repetition of this behaviour. If the bind over is breached, then the criteria would certainly be made out for next time'.

    'I can see the value to this defendant of a supervision requirement to work on the drink problem as you say Mr. W. I can also understand the suggestion by you Mrs. Y of curfew to keep him out of the pub. Why don't we make both requirements, but keep the curfew to the weekends with a shorter supervision period?'

- Call in the legal adviser to advise on any uncertainties on legal or practical points which are raised by the wingers if you need support. This may arise where there is a lack of confidence in using the full range of penalties, e.g. comments such as ...

    'We don't normally do ancillary bind overs in this court - I don't think we should start something new'.

    'If we're thinking of doing a bolt-on ASBO, I think we might need to draw up some requirements - it's probably too complicated'.

    Ask the legal adviser to join you and advise.

4.4.   Self development

4.4.   Engaging in ongoing learning and development

4.4.a. Assessing your own performance against the competence framework. Regularly seeking feedback and identifying your learning and development needs on a continuous basis.

4.4.b. Adapting and developing your own performance in light of changes to law, practice, procedure, research and other developments. Keeping your own resource materials (e.g. bench guide, handbooks, guidelines) up to date.

See: chapter 8. Post-court review and giving and receiving feedback.

- **Identifying own development needs and training**

The MNTI 2 scheme puts greater emphasis on individual magistrates taking responsibility for their own learning and development. This involves undertaking regular self-assessment at the post-sitting review, in addition to preparation for the three-yearly continuation training and appraisal.

Requests for training are now the ultimate responsibility of the Magistrates' Area Training Committee (MATC), via the local Bench Training and Development Committee (BTDC). The membership of the MATC includes a representative of each of the area's BTDCs, a local representative of the Magistrates' Association and the Justices' Clerk with responsibility for training, In the annual programme of meetings the Area Committee will ask each BTDC to list the identified training needs in September. These will be collated, prioritised and actioned as appropriate. Following the demise of the Magistrates' Courts Committees and their responsibility for magistrates' training, the Judicial Studies Board now have a strengthened role in terms of support and monitoring at national level. It is essential to the quality and effectiveness of the training programme that clear requests and suggestions are channelled through post-sitting reviews, appraisals and informal discussion with the BTDC and MATC representatives.

- **Personal learning styles**

The same learning aids are not necessarily the most effective for everyone and it is worth identifying what type of learner we are so that we can tap into the best sources for ourselves. There are four recognised learning styles - activists, reflectors, theorists and pragmatists.

- ☐ Activists - The philosophy of the activist is 'I'll try anything once'. They thrive on new challenges, and enjoy the 'here and now'. They tend to act first and think later.

- ☐ Reflectors - Their response to new information is 'I'd like time to think about this'. They will gather information first and consider all implications before reaching a conclusion. They are good listeners and observers of others and may need encouragement to get involved.

- Theorists - Their philosophy is 'If it's logical it's good'. They think problems through in a logical way and feel uncomfortable with subjective judgements, lateral thinking and anything flippant.

- Pragmatists - Their philosophy is 'if it works it's good'. They search out new ideas, enjoy experiments and like to solve problems. They tend to be impatient with ruminating and open-ended discussions.

This is significant in two ways. About 35% of us fall into one single group, but of the remainder, only 2% of us possess natural attributes across the range. The advantage of the full range is that we would have facility to work methodically through the learning cycle of having an experience, reflecting upon it, drawing theoretical conclusions from it and then pragmatically deciding what changes to take forward. For 98% of us, this is an ideal which does not come naturally and we need to discipline ourselves to act - reflect - draw conclusions and then change accordingly if we are to learn. The post court review and supervised sittings for chairmen are based on this model.

By recognising what type of learner we are, we can pursue 'what comes naturally' in terms of choice of learning methods. The activist may well find it difficult to read and concentrate for lengthy periods, and may learn more from attending discussions and taking an active part in role plays and scenarios. The pragmatist will welcome workbooks, exercises and computer web sites, with real situations rather than unstructured activities. The reflector will be able to engage for long periods with a lecture or video and may feel uncomfortable with spontaneous role play. The theorist is perhaps best suited to reading a variety of materials to stimulate their own views.

Development should ideally touch on all of our senses - each reinforcing the other:

- I hear and I forget
- I see and I remember
- I do and I understand.

Training and development for a magistrate is about being equipped at all times to put justice into practice. The law changes on a daily basis. New options become available. Court practices are constantly revised to create quicker and fairer outcomes. There is only one advocate for the victim who is awaiting the outcome of their unpleasant experience, and the community who are watching the long-term effects. That person is not legally qualified - it is the magistrate. Current knowledge of the options available is essential to make the most of personal life experience in the retiring room. The legal adviser will advise so that the decision is legal, but a well-informed bench will make sure that the decision is also the best.

CHAPTER 5
BAIL

5.1. The general right to unconditional bail

Many cases cannot be dealt with at the first hearing and they are adjourned. Following the decision to adjourn, the adult defendant must be bailed for 'either-way' offences if he has been bailed or produced in custody by the police, and bail must also apply on adjournment of committal proceedings. In other circumstances, it is a matter for the court, e.g. for summary offences, or if the defendant appears on summons for an either way offence.

The starting point is that there is a general right to unconditional bail for all defendants prior to conviction. The right does not therefore apply on committal for sentence or on appeal. However, the right is specifically retained for convicted defendants if the case is adjourned for reports. There are three exceptions to the right to unconditional bail

- **Extradition proceedings**

- **Most serious charges with a previous conviction**

    Exceptional circumstances must be found to justify the grant of bail in respect of those who are charged or convicted of an offence within the list of murder, rape, attempts, or manslaughter, if they have already been convicted of one of the offences.

- **Positive drug test on charge (specific areas only)**

    There is a restriction on bail on those who give a positive drug test on charge (specified areas only) for heroin, cocaine and/or crack cocaine. The test is administered in respect of specific 'trigger offences', e.g. theft, begging and also if there is evidence that drug misuse is the underlying cause of any other offence. If granted bail, the defendant must either agree to a condition of bail to undergo a drug assessment and any proposed follow up treatment. Alternatively they must persuade the court that the alleged offence was not drug-driven and that there is therefore no significant risk that they will commit offences during the bail period. Otherwise they must be remanded in custody

    This is known as the 'Restriction on Bail' (ROB) provision for drug users. Basically the presumption is that the drug user is committing offences to fund his drug habit and that he will continue to do so if bailed, unless he is assessed for drug treatment and participates in any proposed follow up during the bail period. The defendant may or may not ultimately be convicted, and he may or may not be given a community order with a drug rehabilitation requirement, but the drug intervention begins regardless with all the strength of a condition of bail.

N.B. On a broader basis, in all courts, the misuse of controlled substances, is a 'consideration to which the court is to have regard' when considering bail. Outside of the pilot ROB areas, it is merely a factor and is not a bar as such to unconditional bail.

The remainder of defendants must be granted unconditional bail unless one or more of the statutory exceptions to bail apply. Unconditional bail is not a 'soft option'. It does bring with it various obligations and potential actions:

☐ The obligation to attend court (or a police station) at the date and time given

☐ The need to notify the court if a reasonable excuse arises which prevents attendance, e.g. serious illness. If the court is not made aware of a reasonable excuse, then,

☐ Failure to attend will result in a warrant for arrest being issued, and the defendant may be remanded in custody until the case is finalised

☐ Failure to attend will result in an offence of failure to surrender to bail as a separate offence

☐ Any offences committed during the bail period are aggravated in seriousness by the fact that they are committed whilst on bail.

5.2. Statutory exceptions to bail

Specific statutory exceptions must be found. The court must find substantial grounds (reasons) for finding that the exceptions 1 to 3 below do exist. The list below applies to all imprisonable offences and gives examples of reasons.

Statutory exceptions	Substantial grounds (Reasons)
If bailed would: 1. Fail to surrender to custody	• Previous failure to answer bail/comply with bail conditions • Character/ antecedents/lack of community ties • Nature and gravity of offence or breach of order and probable sentence + strength of evidence or character, antecedents etc. above
2. Commit offence on bail	• Previous offences committed on bail • Positive drug test on charge
3. Interfere with witnesses or obstruct the course of justice	• Behaviour/proximity to witnesses

4. Charged with indictable/either-way offence and he was on bail on the date of offence
5. Impracticable to complete inquiries or make the report without keeping defendant in custody
6. Requires custody for own protection, or welfare(child)
7. Not practical to obtain sufficient information to make a bail decision
8. Already serving a sentence of imprisonment
9. Having been released on bail, has been arrested for failing to surrender to custody or breach of bail conditions

5.3. Conditional bail - appropriate conditions and breach

When one or more exceptions apply, the next stage is to consider whether bail conditions would adequately address the exception, or risk. A remand in custody can only be ordered if conditions are properly considered and are considered to be inadequate. The first right is to unconditional bail. The second right is to conditional bail. Conditions may only be added if they are considered to be 'necessary' because of a 'real risk', rather than a 'possible risk'. which every defendant arguably presents to the court.

What exception has been found and can the particular risk be covered adequately by a condition or not? In selecting from the 'standard menu' of conditions or in devising a special condition, there are various factors to consider:

- Does the condition relate directly to the actual exception identified?
- Is it sufficiently clear so that the defendant, the victim and the arresting officer all have exactly the same understanding of what is required? What exactly do they have to do?
- Is it proportionate to the actual risk? The Human Rights Act, Article 8 normally engages in respect of bail conditions as they are restrictions on private life and the restriction must be proportionate in order to comply with the Act. (See chapter 7.5.5.).

Example:

Defendant is charged with being drunk and disorderly and the case is adjourned for trial. There are substantial grounds in the shape of a recent previous conviction for being drunk and disorderly to justify the exception that an offence may be committed on bail. It would be reassuring to impose conditions to report to the local police station every Saturday night and not to enter the city centre for the eight weeks prior to trial.

However, the condition of reporting to the police station is to ensure that the defendant has not absconded and relates to the exception of failing to surrender to the court. This is not made out.

The condition of keeping out of the 'city centre' is unclear in definition. Where does the 'city centre' start and finish?

Also, the conditions impose far too great a restriction and they are disproportionate to the extent of the risk and the relatively minor nature of offending.
The main three exceptions to bail carry a 'normal menu' of conditions as set out below.

5.3.1. Would fail to surrender to court

- To live and sleep at …

This is stronger than a 'residence only' condition which is basically just a mailing address and allows the defendant to go on holiday right through the bail period. 'Live and sleep' means just that, and it takes the address up tariff to a genuine, actually 'living at' address. It will usually be disproportionate to impose a night time curfew in addition, unless there is also concern about further offences being committed during the night.

- To report to … police station between … and … on …

Will this realistically prevent this defendant from absconding? It simply demonstrates that the defendant is in the locality for the 5 minutes of reporting time, but with air travel, he could be out of the country an hour later. Consider the practical aspect of the defendant who uses the opportunity to identify the unmarked police vehicles, plain clothes officers, being legitimately out and about in his target offending area and listening in to police business as he waits to sign on. Consider the resource implication in prioritising interim arrests. It is not an offence to breach a condition and it simply re-opens the question of bail - often re-granted again by the court! When the police ask for a reporting condition through the Crown Prosecution Service they clearly see a value in reporting for this particular defendant and this can be compared to a suggestion which comes instead from the defence.

- To reside at 'approved premises' operated by the probation service or its contractor (previously described as bail hostels) …and to abide by the rules and to reside initially at ……

The initial residence aspect allows the probation service to have flexibility to move the defendant without having to come to court to vary the location if this should become necessary subsequently.

House rules are listed in the National Standards 2005. A normal curfew between 11 p.m. and 6 a.m. unless given express permission to the contrary, A prohibition on using alcohol, solvents or other controlled drugs other than on prescription and following notification to approved premises staff, with a staff power to search rooms and possessions. A management plan will be produced for defendants on bail within 5 working days to ensure relevant support during the bail period. This is an expensive, specialised resource rather than a 'bed for the remand period'. If that is all that your defendant needs, please do not tie the officer's hands to approved premises – leave the suggestions of accommodation open.

- To provide a surety in the sum of ...

The court must consider the financial resources which are actually available, the character of the proposed surety and the residence and relationship proximity. Is it realistic that this person lives near enough and is influential enough towards the defendant to ensure his attendance? It is no longer necessary to find that the defendant may leave the United Kingdom. A warning must be given that the whole sum may be forfeited, dependant upon the culpability of the surety, if the defendant fails to attend.

- To provide a security namely ... cash, passport.

Surrender of passport is now notified immediately by the court to the UK passport office to prevent any application for a duplicate/replacement passport.

5.3.2. Would commit offence whilst on bail

- To live and sleep at .... <u>and</u> to remain indoors at that address between ... and ...

Curfews should only be imposed where there is evidence that offending is likely during the curfew period. Adults can be electronically tagged as part of their bail condition, subject to resources, but this is open to children and young persons only if criteria are satisfied.

The court may additionally make a 'doorstep condition' requiring the defendant to present himself at the door on the request of a police officer in uniform during the curfew period. This is a requirement over and above the restriction of movement and must only be imposed as an extra if it is proportionate to the risk.

- Not to enter ... area where alleged crime committed.

Care is needed to ensure that the area is very clearly defined, and it is not so large as to be disproportionate to the problem or result in 'harmless breaches' because the defendant has genuine reasons to pass through the area, e.g. to visit doctor, solicitor. Smaller areas can usually be more vigorously monitored and are more robustly enforced, e.g. specific car parks, local market area, leisure club changing rooms.

- Not to associate with ... (named persons, usually co-accused).

This condition may be appropriate if the defendant is alleged to have acted in unison with others in committing offences and it is considered likely that their continued association may result in further offending.

- Not to entered licensed public houses and clubs/drink alcohol on the public highway

This may reduce the risk of commission of further offences if it is clear that the defendant tends to commit offences when under the influence of alcohol in public.

5.3.3. Would interfere with witnesses/obstruct the course of justice exceptions

- Not to contact directly or indirectly .... named witnesses.

This condition is particularly useful in domestic violence cases but is one of the most regularly breached conditions in such circumstances. It may be worth reminding the defendant that the condition is there to protect both parties, and if the other party wishes to communicate, they should apply to court for it to be varied or deleted rather than breaking the condition. It is worth checking whether the defendant is already aware of the witnesses' names and/or addresses. If not, then further enquiry should be made to determine whether disclosure is likely to increase the risk of harm.
- Not to enter ... area where witness lives.

This condition can afford some peace of mind to witnesses and may encourage their co-operation. They may be store detectives following a shoplifting charge; victims of burglaries in a particular neighbourhood; licensees of public houses where a disturbance has occurred or victims of domestic violence who simply wish to proceed with their daily life to the local shops and school. It may be helpful to seek representations on your suggested exclusion area definition e.g. exception to pass directly through by vehicle to and from named workplace.

5.3.4. Failing to comply with bail conditions

A defendant may be arrested if a constable has reasonable grounds for believing that the bailee is likely to break any of the conditions of his bail or has reasonable grounds for believing that he has broken any. The defendant must be brought before the court within 24 hours (excluding Sunday etc.) for the breach to be put.

Very importantly, it must be recognised, that the court is not dealing with an offence; there is no proof 'beyond reasonable doubt'; no power to adjourn, and no penalty (unlike the failure to surrender to court where all aspects apply!). If the court is simply 'of the opinion' that the defendant has broken or is likely to break a condition, it may remand him in custody or grant bail as before, or with different conditions. Breach of bail effectively re-opens the whole question of bail and obviously a far greater likelihood of a remand in custody.

5.4. Custody

When the bench find exceptions but cannot safely attach conditions to deal with the risks, then the defendant must be remanded into custody.

At this stage it is worth checking that the court has sufficient information on which to make a full bail decision. The proceedings are inquisitorial which means that there is an onus on the court to ask!
A further statutory exception to bail is that 'the court does not have sufficient information on which to make a decision'. When this is the case e.g. address to be checked out, then the remand must be for the shortest possible period e.g. overnight. A remand in custody before conviction is a serious infringement of liberty and it is wrong to rely on the possibility of a 'stronger application next week' if the decision simply rests upon information which can be obtained overnight. Legal representation must always be offered if a remand in custody is being considered.

The exceptions and reasons must be announced and recorded. The initial maximum period of remand is 8 clear days to custody or 3 days to police cells. A remand to police cells is for the purpose of enquiring into other offences and the defendant must be brought back before the court as soon as that need ceases. In the meantime he must have his detention periodically reviewed under police detention rules.

The period of remand may be extended to 28 days after the 2nd remand in custody. This period is subject to the requirements that the defendant is before the court; that representations are sought from both parties and that care is taken to set a realistic early date for the next stage of the proceedings e.g. for committal.

5.5. Bail for youths

The adult court may deal with the remand of youths under 17, and other remand options are available if exceptions are found to unconditional bail. See chapter 10. Youth Court.

5.6. Bail application procedure

- An application for adjournment is made by prosecution or defence. The Bench determine whether this is appropriate or not.
- Prosecution make representations about any exceptions to bail and substantial grounds if appropriate (exceptions 1 to 3 above). Application may be for remand in custody, or, specific conditions may be suggested. The probation service may have supplied bail information to the parties, e.g. availability of address. (This information may also be passed to other authorities, e.g. to social services if domestic violence poses risk to children).
- Defence application to argue against exceptions put forward if appropriate, or may suggest specific conditions.
- Bench must specify which exceptions are found with reasons, and determine the nature of conditions or whether a remand in custody is necessary.

It is not necessary for evidence to be called and the bail decision is almost invariably made purely on representations and questions from the bench.

5.7. A structured approach to bail

A fair bail decision is critical. The ultimate decision of a remand in custody is available and this is very often based on slim information about a defendant who is not convicted. The decision-making process is about bail risk. It is not about guilt or innocence.

See Bail checklist. Adult Bench Book, 1.21.

The 'ABC' approach is suggested as a structured approach for the decision and for the reasons.

A. Adjournment (or not!)

Should the case be adjourned? The advocates will be aware of the basis for the adjournment and if they have no objection, they will understandably tend to focus their attention on the bail representations. However, the court must first consider carefully whether the case should be adjourned at all. The first question is 'why can't the case proceed?' rather than 'shall we grant bail?' The second question is 'what is the shortest adjournment for specific progress to be made?' rather than 'what date are we adjourning to?'

In any pronouncement, the word adjourn should normally be followed by the reasons and the focus for the next hearing 'because' ..., 'so that' ... and this aspect is part of the decision-making process.

B. Bail

Remember the starting point is the right to unconditional bail for all unconvicted defendants, and those who are adjourned for reports after conviction, with the exception of the most serious charges with record, and positive drug test defendants as described at 8.1.

In order to identify whether any of the exceptions to unconditional bail exist, it is helpful to focus on the features of the offence itself, and then the offender.

- **Offence**

What is alleged by the prosecutor? What is conceded (if anything) by the defence? Is the evidence strong and if so, what is the probable sentence? If it is a lengthy prison sentence, e.g. drug dealing, this may be relevant to finding the exception of failure to surrender. Is there a pattern of offending which is likely to continue e.g. thefts to fund a drug habit, which may found the exception of commission of offences on bail? Is there a reliance on the prosecution witnesses and are they vulnerable? If so can they be adequately protected by conditions or not? Remember that the issue of guilt or innocence is not an issue for a bail decision.

- **Offender**

Is there a history of failure to surrender to bail? This is the most important factor on the record in a bail application. Does the defendant have a stable address? Does he have family/employment commitments? Does he hold a current passport which should be taken as security? Does he have any supporters who are suitable to stand as surety or provide a cash security to the court? What are the explanations/circumstances of any recent failures to attend? Was the defendant on bail at the time of the alleged offence? Was there a positive drug test on charge? If so, the 'ball is in his court' to persuade the court that he will not commit further offences on bail to fund a drug habit.

- **Options (bail)**

If exceptions are not found, then unconditional bail must be granted.
Where there are exceptions with reasons, can they be allayed by relevant conditions?
Define any conditions carefully so that both the defendant and the arresting officer have the same understanding of what they mean?
Check that any conditions are proportionate to the risk.

C. Custody

If exceptions are found and conditions are inadequate, then custody becomes inevitable. (Check with legal adviser that selected exceptions may be used if the offence is non-imprisonable.)

5.8. Failure to surrender to bail

It is an offence to fail to surrender to bail (police or court bail) in criminal proceedings, without reasonable cause. The defence of reasonable cause may, for example be illness or detention elsewhere at the time. It is not a defence to 'get the dates muddled up' - this is simply mitigation.

Alternatively, if there is reasonable cause for failing to attend on the return date, it is also an offence if the defendant fails to surrender 'as soon as reasonably practicable thereafter', i.e. when the medical certificate expired, when he was released from police custody. Both offences carry a maximum of 3 months imprisonment/level 5 fine in the Magistrates' Court and on committal to Crown Court, carry 12 months imprisonment/fine.

- **Procedure**

The procedure is slightly different between police and court bail. Police bail charges are dealt with as for any additional charge and will usually have been charged by the police following arrest on warrant. However, if it is court bail, the prosecutor will consider the matter, often following a brief informal discussion with the defence, and then 'expressly invite' the court to initiate the proceedings. Court bail belongs to the court but it would be inappropriate for the court to both prosecute and adjudicate.
The decision to prosecute rests with the prosecutor effectively, but the court should be vigilant to ensure that the charge is considered by the prosecutor. Whenever the defendant appears in the dock on warrant following a failure to attend on court bail – enquire! This is potentially a very important

conviction for future benches to assess the extent of bail risk and it sends a powerful message that bail really does mean attendance as required. The issue of the warrant and arrest is only the first stage. The offence of failing to attend is quite separate.

- **Dealing with the Failure to Surrender conviction**

The Sentencing Guideline entry point is a community penalty. The Practice Direction requires the offence normally to be dealt with immediately rather than adjourned on with the original offence. If the defendant is bailed, it may be appropriate to impose a short curfew requirement for a few weeks - this will also strengthen the likelihood of attending court for the original offence later! If he is remanded in custody, then the implication is that he may already has convictions for failing to attend and with this aggravation, a short custodial sentence may be imposed immediately to run alongside the remand. A potential lengthy custodial sentence would normally require a full report and may be the exceptional case for adjourning on with the original offence. The Practice Direction states that any custodial sentence should run consecutively to custody for the original offence.

The most obvious mitigation is for the defendant to attend voluntarily at the court or police station as soon as he is aware of the warrant. This is usually prompted by police notification or by solicitor's letter. If there are no similar convictions, the court might consider a short detention in the police cells as the profile of behaviour does not give confidence of disciplined compliance with a court order, e.g. a fine. Unfortunately, the most common situation is that the police are put to the trouble of making an arrest. It is important to emphasise the additional feature of commission of an offence if the defendant is not to see the arrest simply as a taxi ride to court and lunch in the cells!

Failure to surrender to bail is an offence as any other, and reasons must be given for the choice of penalty, together with an appropriate warning as to the option of custody if a further offence is committed.

5.9. Time limits relating to bail

- The maximum period for which someone may be detained without charge or appearance before a court for an arrestable offence is 36 hours, unless a formal extension application is made and granted.

- A defendant who is charged with an offence and kept in custody must be brought before the Magistrates' Court as soon as practicable after being charged, and in any event not later than the first sitting of the court after being charged. For example, if he is charged on Saturday evening, he must be brought before court on Monday (no sittings on Sundays).

- The maximum period for the first two remands in custody is 8 clear days. Thereafter the maximum period is 21 days after conviction and 28 days before conviction if the next stage is fixed.

- The maximum period of remand in custody in respect of indictable offences is 70 days between first appearance and commencement of the committal or trial. The maximum period of remand in custody in respect of offences which are triable summarily is 56 days. Application may be made to 'extend the custody time limits' in specified circumstances, provided that the prosecution have acted with all due diligence and expedition, and application must be made to the court.

5.10. Final points on bail procedures

- Specific reasons must be given if bail is granted in respect of murder, manslaughter and rape e.g. the court is satisfied that the general public are not endangered by the release of the defendant, and the victim is sufficiently protected by the bail conditions.

- A defendant has the right to make two applications which may be based on any argument. Thereafter the court may decline to hear arguments as to fact or law which it has heard previously. The question must be asked 'What is the change of circumstances and how does it relate to the exception(s) found?' Additional application may also be made to a Judge in Chambers based upon a full certificate of refusal by the Magistrates' Court.

- The prosecutor may ask for bail to be reconsidered based upon information which was not available to the court or to the police when the original bail decision was made e.g. a new witness comes forward and the strength of evidence increases substantially.

- Applications may be made to the court to vary conditions of police and court bail at any time e.g. to change address. Always ask for a brief outline of the offence and the details of the surrounding conditions. A variation of a single condition in isolation may sound uncontroversial until it is placed in context e.g. the return home to live with his mother may place the defendant back into the proximity of vulnerable witnesses.

- Applications for bail may be made using live television links with the prison. Representations must be invited if the court intends to proceed in this way, but consent is not required. The defendant must be physically produced in court for sentence and trial.

- The court must give reasons if bail is granted and the prosecutor has opposed bail, e.g. the conditions imposed adequately satisfy the risk presented by the prosecutor. The prosecutor may request a copy of the reasons.

- When bail is granted after opposition, the prosecution may appeal if the offence is imprisonable (s.18). Appeal lies to the Crown Court and oral notice must be given immediately before the defendant is released. Written notice must be given within two hours, otherwise the defendant is released on the bail granted. It will usually be necessary to retire for a short time after the oral notice has been given so that the prosecutor can formulate the written notice of appeal, and the defendant is then remanded in custody for a hearing before a Crown Court Judge within 48 hours.

CHAPTER 6
CASE MANAGEMENT

6.1. Background

One of the main features of the Auld Report in September 2001 was the criticism of the inconsistent and piecemeal way in which cases moved through the criminal justice system. A lot of work has been undertaken as a result to streamline processes and build more effective, timely and responsible liaison between everyone involved in a criminal case. Positive case management procedures were implemented in all criminal cases with effect from 4th April 2005.

These are set out within a single set of Criminal Procedure Rules which govern all courts; a single consolidated Criminal Practice Direction, and a practical Criminal Case Management Framework. The Framework was first produced in July 2004, with a 2nd edition (193 pages) updated to reflect the new rules. It gives practical guidance to all agencies as to who should be doing what, and when, with route maps for each type of case from pre-charge through to appeal.

6.2. Appointment of case progression officers

One of the main practical developments is the requirement under the new Rules which requires the court, and also the prosecution and defence to appoint a named, case progression officer for each case who can be readily contacted during business hours. The officer will monitor compliance with any court directions and respond to any problems with the case going ahead as planned. The Criminal Case Management Framework sets out lists of roles and responsibilities. The examples give just some of the listed duties on one of the agencies at one of the 13 potential stages of a case passing through the Magistrates' Court. They are a helpful indication, particularly for chairmen, as to what information should be available to the court, and what actions should be going on behind the scenes.

Examples:
1. *At the point of charge - prosecution team case progression:*
- *Provide advance information for the defence as soon as practicable following charge, or make available on the morning of the court hearing and ensure that it is served on the defence solicitor if known*
- *Be in a position to deal with plea before venue at the first hearing*
- *Ensure that witness availability has been received*
- *Keep victims and witnesses informed of bail decisions*
- *If required, notify any witnesses of the hearing date after charge*

2. After a 'Not Guilty' plea has been entered - Magistrates' Court case progression:

- Make record of named progression officers for prosecution and defence
- In the event of non-compliance with directions, ascertain the reasons and refer to court for hearing if appropriate
- Set up further hearings as necessary to include progression hearings or pre-trial reviews
- Facilities for video/audio etc. are set up

3. At the point of trial readiness assessment (usually 7-14 days before trial) - defence case progression:

- Ensure all relevant material is copied for the court
- Inform defendant of time and date of hearing and if appropriate, provide a further reminder
- Make any application for adjournment immediately after grounds are known
- Endeavour to ensure defence witnesses are available for trial
- Notify court of any witness requirements and consider involving the witness service
- Comply with any directions made by the court.

6.3. The overriding objective - Criminal Procedure Rules 2005

The practical support is therefore available in a far more defined form than ever before, and the emphasis throughout the Rules and the Framework is that it is the court who should manage the process. The court's role is now discussed.

Rule 1.1. Criminal Procedure Rules 2005 sets this out as follows:

(1) The overriding objective of this new code is that criminal cases be dealt with justly.
(2) Dealing with a criminal case justly includes -
   (a) acquitting the innocent and convicting the guilty;
   (b) dealing with the prosecution and the defence fairly;
   (c) recognising the rights of the defendant, particularly those under Article 6 (see 7.5.)
   (d) respecting the interests of witnesses, victims, jurors and keeping them informed of the progress of the case;
   (e) dealing with the case efficiently and expeditiously;
   (f) ensuring that appropriate information is available to the court when bail and sentence are considered; and
   (g) dealing with the case in ways that take into account - the gravity of the offence alleged - the complexity of what is in issue - the severity of the consequences for the defendant and others affected, and the needs of other cases.

Example:

Compare the case of a disorderly behaviour trial with one police witness, and an assault case with a police witness and also the victim. In both situations the police officer fails to attend on the trial date without a reasonable explanation. In both cases, expedition (e) and the right of the defendant (c) would say that the case must proceed, even though this would mean that the prosecutor would have no alternative but to offer no evidence.

The difference lies in the need to respect the interests of the assault victim (d) for an outcome, e.g. compensation, and also the more serious gravity of offence (g). It _may_ well be 'just' to dismiss the disorderly behaviour as no evidence can be offered, but to consider adjourning the assault matter to another trial date with clear directions for the officer to attend next time.

6.4. The court's case management duties

Rule 3.2 sets out the duties of the court:

(1) The court must further the overriding objective by actively managing the case.
(2) Active case management includes -
    (a) The early identification of the real issues;
    (b) The early identification of the needs of witnesses;
    (c) Achieving certainty as to what must be done, by whom, and when, in particular by the early setting of a timetable for the progress of the case;
    (d) Monitoring the progress of the case and compliance with directions;
    (e) Ensuring that evidence, whether disputed or not, is presented in the shortest and clearest way;
    (f) Discouraging delay, dealing with as many aspects of the case as possible on the same occasion, and avoiding unnecessary hearings;
    (g) Encouraging the participants to co-operate in the progression of the case; and
    (h) Making use of technology.
(3) The court must actively manage the case by giving any directions appropriate to the needs of that case as early as possible.

6.4.1. Making directions

The court is now encouraged to make directions as to what needs to be done, by whom, and by when, in order to satisfy the duties above. Directions may be given on the court's own initiative or on an application by any party, perhaps with a specific proposal. They are relevant and useful from the first hearing, whether a plea is entered or not. Representations should be sought so that timing in particular is realistic.

Example:

A request for CCTV footage should normally provoke a direction as to when it should be served, and then allowing a reasonable time for viewing and instructions before the plea hearing date.

Questions and representations are necessary to make an effective direction. For example: Is it ready to view now? Could it be brought to court? Where is it? Much will depend upon the answers. It will usually be much quicker if it relates to the previous evening in the police cell area as opposed to several weeks ago from a city centre or private camera.

Some periods for directions are based on national or local agreements e.g. direction for committal papers to be served upon defence within 5 weeks and readiness by defence for the committal proceedings in 7 weeks, i.e. 2 weeks to consider the papers.

Directions may be subsequently varied or revoked, and may be used, if necessary, to cancel a hearing. Standard directions are set out for summary trial and the actual committal or transfer to Crown Court.

6.4.2. Case progression form - standard directions for a summary trial

There is now a standard case progression form which includes standard (default) directions for trials in the Magistrates' Court. It identifies full details of the legal representatives and the case progression officers for the court, prosecution and defence. It begins with two questions:

- Has the defendant been advised about credit for pleading guilty? Yes/No.
- Has the defendant been warned that if he is on bail and fails to attend, the proceedings may continue in his absence? Yes/No.

The directions as listed on page 55 will apply unless they are not relevant to the case or if they are specifically varied. For example, some courts require the certificate of trial readiness to be filed at 14 days before trial as the norm, rather than 7 days. Expert evidence may require a longer period depending upon the expertise sought. A record of any directions must be given to the parties. The directions are based upon allowing parties 8 weeks to prepare for trial, or 14 weeks if there is expert evidence.

There is no need to memorise the form and the standard directions, but it is helpful to be aware that it exists and basically what the various requirements are in general terms. Chairmen in particular will then be aware what the expression 'standard directions' means, and be ready for applications to vary them.

So far as defence duties are concerned there are two important points. Firstly, there is no duty for the defence to file a defence statement in the Magistrates' Court (Crown Court only). It is entirely voluntary. In some cases it may be helpful if the defence see an opportunity to avoid the case going to trial if the statement is accepted and the case is then discontinued. It is always worth asking on the trial date whether the defence are prepared to disclose the nature of the defence at that stage if they have not done before. This will assist in note-taking and emphasis.

Secondly, the statutory duty to notify details of witnesses was not brought into force in April 2005 (although it was anticipated).

Prosecution disclosure	Evidence served, including remaining initial disclosure, witness statements, exhibits, tapes, CCTV	28 days from NG plea
Special measures, e.g. video link for child witnesses	Prosecution application Defence to respond within 14 days of service of application	14 days from NG plea
Hearsay/Bad character evidence	Prosecution to serve intention Defence to serve notice opposing Defence to serve intention Prosecution to serve notice opposing	With initial disclosure 14 days - hearsay 7 days - character 14 days of initial disclosure 14 days of receiving notice
Defence statement	Not obligatory - defence choice	14 days of initial disclosure
Defence requiring prosecution witness	Evidence required in person	7 days of prosecution case
Defence serve statements	If defence do not intend to call If required by other party to attend	14 days of prosecution case Notify in 7 days
Written admissions		56 days from NG plea
Expert evidence (does not apply if disclosure may lead to intimidation - grounds must be supplied to other party)	Service of expert report Require attendance/serve own expert evidence Meeting of experts to identify issues if parties agree Notify court if trial length changes	28 days from NG plea 28 days of report 28 days of both reports 14 days of meeting
Point of law	Skeleton argument and authorities	21 days before trial
Trial readiness	Certifies readiness for trial - or not. If problems are identified, an intervention hearing may be arranged by the court case progression officer so that a decision may be reached as to whether the trial should remain in the list or be vacated.	At least 7 days prior to trial

When in force it will bring the additional sanction of the court being able to draw an adverse inference at trial. At the present time, giving full details remains entirely voluntary. However some basic information is ideally required for practical listing purposes. This is the number of prosecution and defence live witnesses with the approximate length of their evidence, and availability dates so that a convenient trial date is booked quickly with a sensible time estimate. This may be fixed at the time of the 'not guilty' plea being entered at the administrative hearing; by subsequent notification to the court progression officer or at a later formal pre-trial review hearing.

The court progression officer will be chasing all directions, e.g. at 21 days before trial to ask the defence/prosecution for the skeleton legal argument to support the defence based on a point of law which they have indicated.

The critical checkpoint lies with the direction to file the certificate of trial readiness - at least 7 days before the trial. If it is revealed that one of the parties is not ready, e.g. a witness is ill or reluctant to attend, or if the certificate is simply not filed at all, then the court progression officer will normally list an intervention/progression hearing. The court may then determine that the trial is to proceed, e.g. witness can be brought to court at a specific time for a limited period only, or a witness summons can be issued in time. Alternatively, the trial may be vacated if appropriate.

6.4.3. Case progression forms - cases committed to the Crown Court

On the same basis, standard directions are also set out for cases which are 'committed for trial' or 'sent' to the Crown Court, This means that the Magistrates' Court now makes orders which affect the case progression at Crown Court. The significant action point is to fix the next hearing date for Crown Court. This will be a 'plea and case management' hearing for cases which are committed for trial. This should be fixed within about 7 weeks in committal for trial cases.

When cases are 'sent' to the Crown Court, i.e. indictable only matters, then the next hearing may be an earlier 'preliminary hearing' within about 14 days, e.g. if a guilty plea is anticipated, or a defendant is a young person. Normally they will be listed for a 'plea and case management' hearing, but in a longer time frame than the committal cases - within about 14 weeks if in custody.

6.4.4. Sanctions

- Case to proceed

When realistic directions are made, and they are not complied with, the presumption is that the case will go ahead in any event, unless there is a good reason for the failure to comply. Neither party wants to find themselves in a situation at trial date where the case is ordered to proceed and they cannot offer the evidence they had intended, because it has not been served properly in advance, or a witness has not been adequately notified or summoned to attend. The end result for a prosecution would be a dismissal of the case on the basis of 'no evidence offered'. This can also arise if a case is directed to proceed as a committal if papers are not ready, when the outcome would again be 'no evidence offered' and the case would be discharged. (Note that a discharge at committal stage does not prevent the defendant being re-charged).

There is an incentive to comply with directions, but only if they are expected to be taken seriously! If cases are routinely adjourned for oversights and failures to check actions and supply evidence, then directions will lose their value in that court.

- Wasted costs

When the court is satisfied that costs have been incurred by one of the parties as a result of an unnecessary or improper act or omission by another party, the court may order that all or part of those costs incurred are paid. For example, the defendant has not attended to give instructions to his solicitor and the trial is adjourned, he may be made responsible for the prosecution costs for the day, even if he is ultimately acquitted of the offence.

The court may also disallow or order a legal representative to meet the whole or part of any wasted costs which are incurred as a result of any improper, unreasonable or negligent act or omission on the part of the legal representative or his employee. The order against a legal representative is draconian and the court must formally state the grounds of its complaint, and a transcript of the wasted costs hearing must be made.

Representations must be sought before making a costs order and the sum must be specified.

- Notification to authorities of serious failures to comply

Serious or repetitive failures may be notified to the Local Criminal Justice Board in respect of the police and CPS, and to the Legal Services Commission in respect of defence failures to comply without reasonable excuse.

6.5. Effective case management - before and after plea

6.5.1. Advance information served at first opportunity

An indication of plea is the expectation on the first hearing. Advance information should therefore be provided to the defendant as soon as practicable after charge, so that he can understand the nature of the case against him. This is sometimes served as late as the day of the hearing. It may be handed directly to the defendant or to the defence solicitor, preferably before the case is to be called, so that instructions can be taken without having to stand the case down later. If a warrant has been issued, the advance information will normally be attached to the court file or be available via the local probation team for community order breach cases, so that it can be served in court after arrest. Adjournments for plea, even after a warrant has been executed, should therefore be limited to the few cases where the advance information is lengthy or complex. When something is missing and an adjournment is necessary, consider a specific direction for the party to supply in the shortest reasonable time frame, with time for instructions to be taken before the next hearing.

6.5.2. The 'must proceed next time' direction

Directions are often invited on the lines of 'A direction that the case must proceed next time'. Such directions are both counter-productive and pointless - all cases should proceed as directed next time! By adding the direction to some cases and not to others, there is an inference that, without the direction there is always a fighting chance of getting a final adjournment e.g. a respectful acknowledgement that this really is the last opportunity to prepare committal papers.

Also, it actually counts for very little as every application must be dealt with on the information on the day if justice is to be achieved. A refusal to adjourn a case because the previous bench had stated that no further adjournments would be allowed was overturned on appeal. The court said that the comments of the previous bench were relevant to the decision but all factors had to be considered and the previous statement was not binding on a subsequent bench who had a duty to exercise their own judicial discretion (R v Aberdare Justices ex.p DPP 1990). A specific direction as to particular action to be undertaken focuses the application on exactly what steps have been taken. A fair decision can then be reached as to whether, for instance, the committal is further adjourned for the additional statements, or the case is discharged because the evidence cannot be offered.

6.5.3. Adjournments for pre-sentence reports

The greatest potential for delay is when such a case is adjourned unnecessarily for a standard full pre-sentence report after a guilty plea. If an application is made for reports consider the questions first:

- What is the entry point for the offence?
- Is there anything in the prosecution outline to aggravate seriousness?
- Does the level of seriousness merit a community order?
- If so, does the level/intended requirement lend itself to a fast delivery report e.g. low level order, or unpaid work/supervision/curfew at any level. If so, stand the case down or adjourn for the shorter period required.
- Are there any special factors which would require a standard delivery report e.g. domestic violence, mental illness. If so, a standard report will be required so that risk can be assessed.
- If the offence falls within the 'so serious' level, is there a recent report, or is a report 'unnecessary' for sentence today, e.g. previous custodial penalties and only a short custodial period is appropriate?
- Is seriousness above Magistrates' Court sentencing powers? If so, seek representations on whether the case should be committed for sentence forthwith.

Always pause and consider before agreeing to an application for a full standard report. The fast delivery report has been invented to avoid this delay and unnecessary resource, either by standing down on the day, or within

5 days. Any form of report may be unnecessary for serious offenders who may possibly be sentenced without a new report, or more significantly, they should be committed to Crown Court immediately. Case management runs all the way to sentencing at the earliest possible opportunity.

6.6. Effective trial management

In terms of case management, the adjournment of a trial creates problems, because of the wasted court time, the inconvenience to witnesses, and the delay caused to both the defendant and the victim. The national statistics on trial completion at first hearing does not present a satisfactory picture - about 1 in 3 trials actually go ahead.

Terminology first. There are four potential outcomes for every trial:

- An *'effective'* trial proceeds on the day to verdict. The best outcome.
- An *'ineffective'* trial is when expected progress is not made due to action by one of more of the prosecution, the defence or the court and a further listing for trial is required. The worst outcome.
- A *'cracked'* trial may occur when the defendant makes a late plea change or pleads guilty to an alternative or is bound over i.e. there is a 'result'. The shame is that this did not happen earlier, but at least there is a result.
- A *'cracked'* trial may alternatively occur if the prosecution either offers no evidence or ends the case because a witness is absent or has withdrawn or the defendant is found unfit to plead, i.e. no 'result'. There is a multitude of reasons why this will always happen in some cases.

The focus is most heavily on reducing 'ineffective' trials and The Public Service Agreement target is to reduce ineffective trials in the Magistrates' Court to 23% by March 2006.

Applications are usually based on a limited range of scenarios and some suggested questions and outcomes are suggested below, in order to identify whether it is 'just' to proceed or adjourn.

6.6.1. Adjournment of a trial - the absent witness

The big 'no' question is, 'Is this witness important?' The answer is highly unlikely to be 'No - on reflection - not really important at all.' Better to identify whether the court believes that they are so important that it would not be 'just' to go ahead without them.

- *What material evidence does the witness contribute to the case?*
- *How is it significant to the defence?*
- *Is he the only witness supplying this particular evidence?*
- *Was this witness listed by name (not obligatory) or as one of the number of witnesses?*
- *When/how was he told of the hearing date?*
- *When was it discovered that he would not be attending?*
- *Why didn't the party apply for a witness summons to secure attendance?(see below).*

- *Can he be contacted by telephone today?*
- *Has he supplied a witness statement, or been interviewed by the defence? When?*
- *Ask for representations on proceeding in the absence of the witness.*
- *Ask for representations on part-hearing the case.*

The greater the effort to identify his existence, secure his attendance, and obtain his witness statement the more likely that he is genuinely considered to play a vital part.

A witness summons may be issued if the person is likely to be able to give material evidence and it is in the interests of justice to do so. Since August 2005 it is no longer necessary to demonstrate that the person will not attend voluntarily.

6.6.2. Adjournment of a trial - the absent defendant

- *What reasons, if any, are given for the non-attendance?*
- *What is the case history, including the bail history?*
- *Did the defendant attend the pre-trial review hearing?*
- *When, if at all, did he give instructions for the trial to his solicitor?*
- *Check the answer to the question on the standard directions form: Has the defendant been warned that if he is on bail and fails to attend, the proceedings may continue in his absence? The bench should also have given the warning at the previous hearing.*

Clearly it is important to take every step to ensure that the defendant is allowed to participate effectively in the case and presence at the trial is the ideal, but this is not an absolute right. A denial would otherwise be an easy way to avoid the case proceeding - simply never attend court! An amendment to the Trials in Absence Direction was handed down by the Lord Chief Justice in January 2004 and reads as follows:

'A defendant has a right, in general, to be present and to be represented at his trial. However, a defendant may choose not to exercise those rights by voluntarily absenting himself and failing to instruct his lawyers adequately so that they can represent him. In the case of proceedings before the Magistrates' Court, there is an express statutory power to hear trials in the defendant's absence (s.11 Magistrates' Courts Act 1980). In such circumstances, the court has discretion whether the trial should take place in his/her absence.

Generally the approach should be to proceed with the trial in the defendant's absence if a warrant is justified, i.e. there is no apparent reasonable excuse for failing to attend court. The issue of a warrant and the adjournment of the trial simply do not fit together in logic. When witnesses are present and the case is ready to proceed - hear it, and then if necessary issue the warrant after conviction if the defendant is required to attend for sentence.

What if the defendant has had an accident on the way to court? This can be dealt with justly under the re-opening provisions in the interests of justice if so required. Similarly, the right to appeal against conviction/sentence will lie to the Crown Court whether the defendant was present or not. All is not lost.

CHAPTER 7
PROCEDURE AND EVIDENCE

PROCEDURE

7.1. The doctrine of precedent

A basic awareness of the court hierarchy is helpful to understand where the Magistrates' Court sits in the big picture and the significance of the hierarchy. Whilst the main source of our law is found in legislation i.e. Acts of Parliament and rules, a large body of law is also created by judges in the course of deciding cases. The decisions of the higher courts bind the lower courts. This is known as the 'doctrine of precedent'. Many of the decisions are determinations of how legislation should be interpreted in the circumstances of a particular case. Appeal lies generally from the lower courts and up through the higher courts.

The court hierarchy (in descending order)

- **The European Court of Human Rights** sits in Strasbourg and deals with Human Rights issues. Any individual, non-governmental organisation or group of individuals can petition the court, alleging a violation of Human Rights.

- **The House of Lords** is the ultimate domestic appeal court which deals with appeals on points of law which involve matters of public importance. For example, defining significant words in a statute. It also makes decisions where new issues arise, e.g. to determine that a girl under 16 did not need parental consent to be given contraceptive services.

- **The Court of Appeal** lies 'below' the House of Lords in the hierarchy. The appeal hearing is merely a review of the lower court's decision, but fresh evidence may be admitted and a retrial may be allowed if it is in the interests of justice to do. On a criminal matter, the High Court must first certify that a point of law of general public importance is involved in the decision and leave must be given for the appeal.

- **The High Court** is made up of three divisions. Criminal matters are dealt with in the Queens Bench Division, and it is presided over by the Lord Chief Justice. Trials in the High Court are heard either in London or in one of the provincial trial centres.

  Appeals to the High Court can go straight from the Magistrates' Court, or via the Crown Court. There are two types which magistrates are likely to be involved with. Firstly, an appeal 'by way of case stated'. The proceedings are questioned on the ground that it is wrong in law or in excess of jurisdiction, and the magistrates are asked to state a case for the opinion of the High Court. The legal adviser will usually draft this out for approval and signature. The appeal is heard by two or three judges who hear counsel from each side.

Secondly, there is an 'application for judicial review' which is limited to considering whether the Magistrates' Court has failed to exercise its jurisdiction properly or whether it has come to some error of law which appears on the face of the record. It challenges process rather than the actual decision. Leave must be obtained from a High Court judge that there is an arguable case.

- **The Crown Court** is a single court which can sit anywhere in England and Wales. Sittings are usually confined to the towns designated as court centres. When the Crown Court sits in the city of London, it is known as the Central Criminal Court - often referred to as the Old Bailey. It deals with trials on indictment before a judge and jury; criminal appeals from Magistrates' Court against conviction and/or sentence; cases committed for greater sentence than the magistrates may impose, and it also has a very limited civil jurisdiction.

  Appeal against conviction from the Magistrates' Court is based on fact only, ranging from disputed identity through to whether the defendant had the requisite intention to steal the property or not. Dealing with an appeal involves rehearing the case. The parties are not confined to the evidence given in the Magistrates' Court. Between two and four magistrates sit on appeals to the Crown Court, depending upon the type of case, along with the judge or recorder. The decision is that of the majority on the bench and the magistrates carry equal weight with the professional judge, unless a casting vote is required. The judge or recorder presides and his rulings on legal matters bind the magistrates.

  Appeal may also be made against sentence alone. The Crown Court will give reasons for the decision and the magistrates involved in the original case are entitled to see the reasons. Sentence may well be increased as well as reduced on appeal.

The decisions of the above courts are binding on the Magistrates' Court, provided that they are compatible with the Human Rights Act.

- **The County Court** deals solely with civil matters e.g., adoption, divorce, claims for compensation. Claims for higher amounts are dealt with in the High Court. The compensation claims may well arise out of criminal matters which came before the Magistrates' Court if compensation is not awarded, or is not collected by the Magistrates' Court, e.g. traffic accidents, health and safety matters, serious criminal injuries.

7.2. Criminal and Civil cases - the differences

Criminal cases involve acts against the rules of the community at large and the state. The Crown Prosecution Service will normally (but not exclusively) take action against the offender.

The most common offences are listed below, along with the legislation (Act of Parliament)) which created them:

- Theft Act 1968 – theft, robbery, burglary, handling stolen goods, taking a motor vehicle without consent, going equipped for theft, deception
- Public Order Act 1986 – violent disorder, affray, causing likely harassment, alarm or distress (disorderly behaviour), intending to cause harassment, alarm or distress
- Road Traffic Acts – dangerous driving, speeding, no insurance
- Offences against the Person Act 1861 – assault occasioning actual bodily harm, wounding
- Criminal Justice Act 1988 - common assault
- Misuse of Drugs Act 1971 – possession and supply of illegal drugs e.g. ecstasy, heroin, cannabis
- Criminal Damage Act 1971 – criminal damage and arson.

The statute gives the definition of the various offences and the maximum penalties. Rules, regulations and case law from the higher courts further interpret the law.

Civil cases are based upon specific relationships. This may between individuals or between an individual and a corporation, and the court's role is to settle disputes and make formal orders between the parties. In the Magistrates' Court the vast majority of civil cases are heard in the family proceedings court. There are also specific civil cases, e.g. applications by local authorities for ASBOs, and a diminished role now in licensing cases.

7.3. The standard and burden of proof in criminal and civil cases

Criminal cases	**Civil cases**
Terminology: The prosecutor prosecutes the defendant or accused.	Terminology: The complainant/plaintiff sues, or complains or brings an action against the defendant or respondent.
The defendant is found guilty/ convicted	An order is made against the defendant/respondent if the case is proved.
The evidential burden of proof is on the prosecutor.	The evidential burden of proof is on the complainant/plaintiff.
Standard of proof is to 'prove beyond reasonable doubt'. This does not mean beyond a shadow of a doubt.	Standard of proof is to prove on balance of probabilities - 'being more probable than not'. (Note the exception of a civil application for an ASBO which requires proof 'beyond reasonable doubt').

7.4. The order of proceedings in criminal and civil cases

Criminal cases	Civil cases
Order of evidence and speeches (disputed matter):	Order of evidence and speeches:
Prosecutor may address the court. Prosecution evidence. Defendant may address, whether or not he afterwards calls evidence. Prosecutor evidence to rebut defence evidence. Defendant may address <u>if</u> he has not done so already (usually left to this point). Either party may address a 2nd time with leave of the court. If both address the court twice, the <u>accused</u> has the last word.	Complainant may address the court. Complainant's evidence. Defendant may address, whether or not he afterwards calls evidence. Complainant evidence to rebut defence evidence. Defendant may address if he has not done so already. Either party may address a 2nd time with leave of the court. If both address the court twice, the <u>complainant</u> has the last word.

7.5. The Human Rights Act 1998 - the effect in the Magistrates' Court

The Act encapsulates the rights and freedoms of the European Convention on Human Rights and Freedoms agreed in 1950, and brings them into our domestic law, along with the case law which has built up under the Convention. Domestic courts must take into account the judgements, decisions, declarations and opinions of the European Court of Human Rights based in Strasbourg. Whilst this is a potentially complex topic area, the reality is that only two Convention Articles tend to be quoted in the Magistrates' Court and the issues are relatively straightforward. Whilst points are sometimes taken in the spirit of 'human rights', the detail is often found in other legislation or case law. The relevant Articles are discussed below, along with the associated legal provisions which also relate to the points discussed.

- Article 6 - the right to a fair trial, and specific provisions in relation to criminal matters
- Article 8 - the right to respect for private and family life.

7.5.1. Article 6 - The right to a fair trial

'Everyone is entitled to a fair and public hearing within a reasonable time by an independent and impartial tribunal established by law. The judgement shall be pronounced publicly unless exceptions apply.'

Taking each of the aspects in turn. So far as impartiality is concerned, this is covered by statute law and by case law which goes back to 1924, stating;

'It is not merely of some importance but is of fundamental importance that justice should not only be done but should manifestly and undoubtedly be seen to be done.'

The situations below indicate when a magistrate may not be regarded as being 'impartial' and they should not therefore adjudicate in a particular case:

7.5.2. 'Impartial tribunal' - disqualification from sitting and conflict of interest

'Justice being seen to be done' is the key. It is not about whether there actually is bias, but in certain situations, a magistrate should notify the chairman immediately so that they may withdraw from the bench.

- Members of a local authority must not sit on any cases brought by or against the authority, or by way of an appeal from a decision of the authority or an officer of the authority.

- Magistrates who have dealt with a bail application and considered previous convictions must not sit on a trial of the same defendant in the same proceedings. Similarly magistrates should not sit on a trial if they have dealt with an application for a representation order which has detailed the previous convictions unless they are formally before the trial court as evidence of bad character.

- If a magistrate has a direct pecuniary interest, however small, or a proprietary interest in the outcome of the case, then he is sitting as a 'judge in his own cause' and is disqualified, e.g. owning shares in a company which is before the court.

- A magistrate should not sit on a case if there is 'apparent bias'. The test is whether the circumstances would lead a fair-minded and informed observer to conclude that there was a real possibility that the tribunal was biased. 'Apparent bias' means that the magistrate might unfairly regard with favour or disfavour the case of a party to the issue under consideration, e.g. a magistrate is married to the prosecutor, or is the next door neighbour of the defendant or witness. Particularly in a rural community or in the case of schoolteachers who 'know' many people, a practical test is whether the magistrate would invite the person into their house for a cup of tea, as opposed to simply knowing their name and exchanging pleasantries. If there are legitimate reasons to fear impartiality, a magistrate must withdraw. Basically if someone in the public gallery was aware of the relationship could they reasonably fear that there could be a biased decision?

7.5.3. Article 6 - Judgement to be 'pronounced publicly' - Press restrictions

There is a general obligation on the court to give reasons for judgements in the spirit of a fair trial so that both the defendant and the public know the basis of the decision. There is also a specific statutory requirement to give reasons in certain situations in any event e.g. upon refusal of bail, imposition of custody, when refusing to order compensation, when finding special reasons for not endorsing a licence.

The test for adequacy of reasons is whether a person with notice of all the facts and representations made to the court would be able to understand the basis of the decision including the conclusions reached by the court on disputed facts or contentious submissions.

The Press may attend the adult court and may report freely on what they hear unless legal exceptions apply or the court makes restrictions. The principle exception is in both youth and family courts where reporting is generally prohibited as a starting point. In the adult court, the starting point is full publicity unless one of the exceptions below applies and an order is made to restrict publicity:

The most often used statutory press restriction relates to children and young people in the adult court:
'The court may direct that no report shall reveal the name, address or school, or include any particulars calculated to lead to the identification of a child or young person <u>concerned</u> in the proceedings. This may be either as being the person by or against or in respect of whom the proceedings are being taken, or as a being a witness therein' (s.39 Children and Young Persons Act 1933). Publication in contravention of such a direction carries a level 5 fine.

There must be reasons to outweigh the legitimate interests of the public in receiving fair reports of the proceedings and knowing the identity of those in the community who have been guilty of criminal conduct. Publicity must never be regarded as being part of the punishment.

Examples of possible restrictions on identification:

1. Protection of the child's identity if the parent are convicted for failing to send the child to school. By giving the parent's name and the school, the child would be identified.

2. Protection of a young person who is made the subject of an Anti Social Behaviour Order (ASBO) in the adult court. As an ASBO is a civil application it cannot be heard in the youth court. Interestingly, the usual bar on publicity in youth court proceedings does not apply to bolt-on ASBOs in youth court in criminal proceedings, and breach proceedings.

Various matters must be considered before making a publicity restriction order. In considering an ASBO application, the court should consider such matters as:

- Does the local community need to know who the order is made against and what the actual conditions are, so that they can report any breaches to the police? If there are only a few people affected by the order then it may be more appropriate for the police to personally notify them. If a larger section of the community is affected then this would not be practical.

- Is the order of little real benefit to the victims of the behaviour unless it is well publicised?
- Are the risks of publicity for the defendant proportionate to the need to protect others?
- Should there be a Press restriction whilst a disputed youth ASBO case is heard because it may ultimately be dismissed? Should it be reconsidered if the case is found proved so that details can be published?

Press restriction powers also apply in the Magistrates' Court in respect of sexual offences where generally no material should be published to identify the victim and also limitation of details in respect of committal proceedings unless Press restrictions are raised.

Submissions should always be sought from the parties and the Press if the court intends to exclude the Press or restrict reporting in any way. The general criteria will always be whether it is in the interests of justice to restrict the information reaching the public or not. The precise terms of the restriction must be announced - normally it is names and anything which could lead to the identity being discovered - be clear in open court and in written form - because 'something' is likely to be reported.

7.5.4. Article 6 - specific provisions relating to criminal offences

Some provisions of Article 6 apply only to criminal proceedings in order to give greater protection than in civil proceedings. For these purposes, 'criminal' proceedings extend to cases where the party could face custody even though they would not normally be classed as criminal proceedings e.g. non-payment of council tax.

- 'Everyone charged with a criminal offence is presumed innocent until proved guilty according to law.

And the rights:

- To be informed promptly and in a language which he understands, the nature and cause of the accusation against him.
- To defend himself in person or through legal assistance of his own choosing, or have free legal assistance if of insufficient means and the interests of justice so require.
- To time (and confidential) facilities to prepare defence.
- To examine or have examined witnesses against him and to obtain the attendance and examination of witnesses on his behalf under the same conditions as witnesses against him.
- To have the free assistance of an interpreter if he cannot understand or speak the language used in court.' (The court is under an obligation to provide an interpreter to the defendant when this is necessary, without any cost to the defendant regardless of his means).

7.5.5. Article 8 - The right to respect for private and family life

(1) *'Everyone has the right to respect for his private and family life, his home and his correspondence.*

(2) *There shall be no interference by a public authority with the exercise of this right unless it is accordance with the law and is necessary ... for the prevention of disorder or crime, for the protection of health and morals, or for the protection of the rights and freedoms of others.'*

This is known as a qualified right. Basically we have the right to do as we please in our private lives but we may be restricted in this to whatever extent is necessary to prevent disorder and crime or to protect the rights and freedoms of others.

This right 'engages' with virtually every bail condition and with every sentence of the court. There will almost inevitably be some interference with the defendant's private life. From having to remain indoors under a curfew to the ultimate restriction on liberty with a custodial sentence. From being excluded from a particular area under an ASBO through to having to spend money on a fine instead of private life.

There are three requirements to consider whenever imposing a restriction on a qualified right, and they must be applied in respect of bail and sentence restrictions:

- Is it lawful? Yes, it will be as all bail restrictions and sentences derive from clear, accessible legal criteria and limitations.
- Does it pursue one of the legitimate aims? Yes, it will do as all bail restrictions and sentencing will be imposed in order to prevent disorder and crime, or protect the rights and freedoms of others.
- Is it no more than is necessary in a democratic society? This is the 'one to watch'. The nature of the restriction must be proportionate to the problem and not a 'sledgehammer to crack a nut'. For example it may well be lawful and legitimate to impose a six month night-time curfew requirement on a defendant found guilty of drunk and disorderly, but it would be wholly disproportionate to the charge.

The expression, 'proportionate' is regularly quoted by advocates and it is a shorthand reference to the requirement of Article 8, which does not allow for 'over the top' restrictions on a defendant, even if the statute allows the penalty in law.

7.6. Types of criminal offences and relevant procedures

7.6.1. 'Indictable only' offences

These are the most serious offences which may only be dealt with by the Crown Court, e.g. murder, rape, robbery. They are brought before the Magistrates' Court as new charges and then 'sent' to the Crown Court along with any other qualifying offences. No plea is entered in the Magistrates' Court, but bail must be dealt with for the period between appearance in the Magistrates' Court and the next hearing at the Crown Court. A 'preliminary hearing' will be fixed in some cases in about 14 days, e.g. if a guilty plea is anticipated, or a 'plea and case management' hearing in about 14 weeks if the defendant is in custody.

7.6.2. 'Summary' offences

These are offences which may only be dealt with in the Magistrates' Court, e.g. common assault, taking a motor vehicle without the owner's consent, driving whilst disqualified. The charge is read out by the legal adviser and the defendant is simply asked whether he pleads 'guilty' or 'not guilty'.

Following a guilty plea, the prosecutor outlines the circumstances of the offence and produces any offences to be taken into consideration, any previous convictions and makes any applications, e.g. for compensation. The defendant or his solicitor then gives the defence version of events and mitigates. The court then determines whether to sentence immediately or obtain a probation report to assist in determining penalty.

- **Cases dealt with in the absence of the defendant**

Many 'summary only' matters are dealt with in the absence of the defendant. For example, speeding, not having a television licence, driving without insurance, The court either hears a summary, or full witness statements are read out. Any statements must have been sent to the defendant at least 8 working days before the hearing. If the case is found proved in absence, the court may proceed to sentence. Sometimes the defendant admits the offence in writing or sends written mitigation and full details of means to the court so that a fair fine may be assessed. Sometimes the defendant does not respond at all. In the case of endorseable traffic offences, the court will have obtained 'a print out' of any previous driving convictions from the DVLA at Swansea (in the likely event that the defendant does not send his licence to the court!), and the fine must be fixed arbitrarily.

When the notice of fine is received the defendant may say that he had not received the original summons and was unaware of the proceedings. He can then make a statutory declaration to this effect and the conviction is quashed with the option of a fresh summons being issued. Alternatively he may admit the matter but argue that the fine is far too high for his income, and in these circumstances, the court may rectify the figure to a fair amount on the actual means - a regular scenario in fine default court.

See chapter 8.49. Speed camera offences.

7.6.3. 'Either-way' offences and 'mode of trial'

These are offences which may be dealt with by the Magistrates' Court or the Crown Court, e.g. theft, burglary, assault occasioning actual bodily harm. Such offences carry higher penalties in the Crown Court. The defendant is entitled to receive details of the prosecution case against him before indicating his plea. This is known as 'Advance Information'. It consists of either, the written statements which the prosecutor intends to give as evidence or, a summary of the facts which are to be read out.

The court must be satisfied that the defendant is aware of his right to ask for advance information, and has had time to consider it. The procedure is explained by the legal adviser who warns that the magistrates may commit the case to the Crown Court on conviction if they consider that their sentencing powers are insufficient after hearing all the facts. The charge is read out, and the defendant is asked for indication of his plea, 'guilty' or 'not guilty'. or 'no indication of plea'.

- **'Guilty' plea indication**

When a 'guilty' plea is indicated, the case then proceeds as for a summary offence - prosecution outline, followed by defence, as described above. The big difference is that the court must decide whether its powers are actually sufficient before moving into sentencing. The defence must always be given the opportunity to respond if the court considers that the case should be committed for sentence to the Crown Court. Committal to Crown Court 'for sentence' may then follow immediately if appropriate.

- **'Newton hearing'**

Evidence is not formally given if there is a guilty plea with one exception. This is when there is a fundamental difference between the prosecution version of events and the defence version which could affect sentence. For example, the defendant pleads guilty to assault on the basis of a single slap to the face, but the prosecution version is that there were several blows with a weapon. In such cases, evidence is called after the guilty plea in order to determine which version of events the court will sentence upon. In this scenario, whether to a community order on the lesser version of events or to custody if the more serious version is accepted. This is known as a 'Newton hearing'. A Newton hearing is not required just because there are differences in the versions of events - we would have many such cases. It is because those differences are so great that the sentence would be different.

- **'Not guilty' plea or no indication and 'mode of trial'**

The prosecution are normally aware in advance of cases where a 'not guilty' plea is anticipated. This becomes clear when the Crown Prosecutor considers the police evidence including any defence response on charge and interview, when they assess the evidence to determine the most appropriate charge. These cases are listed as 'early administrative hearings' rather than 'early first hearings' where the anticipated guilty pleas are destined.

The hearing is largely administrative and procedural in order to set the anticipated trial en route either to the Magistrates' Court or the Crown Court and it is recognised that it will not be going ahead to conclusion on first listing.

The defendant is asked to indicate his plea - 'not guilty', or he may choose to enter no plea at all. The court hears representations from the prosecution about the seriousness of the case so that the court can assess whether the Magistrates' Court powers are sufficient. This is known as determining 'mode of trial'. For this purpose, the court should assume that the prosecution version is correct, e.g. value of goods stolen, that a weapon was used, even though this is denied.

In order to assist in the decision, the Sentencing Guidelines set out entry points.

Examples:

- *Burglary (dwelling) - Committal to Crown Court, compared to*
- *Burglary (non-dwelling) - Magistrates' Court - community penalty.*
- *Supply of drugs - Crown Court, compared to*
- *Possession of class A drugs - Magistrates' Court - community penalty.*
- *Possess indecent photographs - Crown Court.*

There is further guidance in the National Mode of Trial Guidelines which are found in Section 2 of the Adult Bench Book.

Example:

Burglary (non-dwelling). Entry point - Magistrates' Court - community penalty. Cases should be tried summarily <u>unless</u> the court considers that one or more of the following features is present in the case and that its sentencing powers are insufficient.

1. *Entry of a pharmacy or doctor's surgery.*
2. *Fear is caused or violence is done to anyone lawfully on the premises.*
3. *The offence has professional hallmarks.*
4. *Vandalism on a substantial scale.*
5. *The un-recovered property is of a high value.*

Where cases involve complex questions of fact or difficult questions of law, committal should be considered.

The defence also make representations on the 'mode of trial' and the court then determines whether the case is suitable for summary trial in the Magistrates' Court or not. If it is suitable, and the defendant agrees, it is adjourned for pre-trial review or straight to a trial date in the Magistrates' Court. Appropriate directions are made to ensure that the preparation for trial timetable is in place (See 6.4.2.).

If is not considered suitable, i.e. it is too serious, the case is adjourned for statements to be prepared for later committal to the Crown Court 'for trial'.

- **Committal for trial of either-way offence**

The case is committed for trial therefore if the magistrates feel that their powers are insufficient - summary trial is not appropriate. If the court does accept jurisdiction, the defendant has the right, in any event, to elect trial at Crown Court on his own choice because the offence is 'either-way' e.g. theft of a bar of chocolate can be tried at Crown Court if the defendant so chooses. The case can only be committed if the statements disclose that there is sufficient evidence to put the defendant on trial. This is known as a 'prima facie' case - not beyond reasonable doubt as the full trial will require - just a case to be answered.

The defence usually concede that there is a 'prima facie' case and the statements are simply handed in to the court. Occasionally the Magistrates' Court is required to consider the evidence, and if so determined, the court then commits the defendant to Crown Court.
The committal hearing also involves giving standard directions (see 6.4.3.); fixing a 'plea and case management' hearing date at Crown Court; extending the legal representation order to Crown Court if appropriate and warning that notice is required if any witnesses are required to attend in person at the Crown Court.

If a 'prima facie' case is not made out, then the case is 'discharged'. Similarly, if the court refuse to adjourn a committal case for the evidence to be prepared, then it will 'discharge' the case, but this does not prevent the defendant being re-charged when the full evidence is obtained. Committal discharge is not the same as a finding of not guilty!

Where there are two or more defendants who are jointly charged, each individual has the right to elect trial by jury.

7.7. Criminal trial - sequence of events

The trial process is as follows:

- **Prosecution opening**

Before the prosecution begins, all witnesses must be cleared from the court to wait outside the court until called to give their evidence, so that each witness is heard to be giving their own independent recollection, rather than building on what someone else has said.

The prosecution case in a criminal matter must be proved beyond reasonable doubt and the initial outline will give the basis on which the proof will be given. At this stage the prosecutor normally describes what is alleged to have happened and how it is intended to prove the various elements of the offence.

It is recommended that magistrates refrain from taking detailed notes at this point so that there is no appearance of the case being decided upon representations rather than on actual evidence. Obviously it is helpful to get a feel for the case and in particular to identify any potential line of defence e.g. mistaken identity, self-defence. This highlights the evidence which must be noted carefully.

- **Prosecution case**

Undisputed, but material evidence may simply be read from statements,

Example:

A statement from the owner of a stolen motor car - 'I was the owner of vehicle registered XXX 333. I parked the car in the YY car park, next to the bottle bank at about 7 p.m. on the 1st May. I went into the SS supermarket and when I returned at about 8 p.m. my car was not there. No one else had any right to take my car'.

No dispute, but the facts are material to the case.

- **Examination in chief**

The party who is calling the witness conducts the 'examination in chief'. The prosecutor therefore examines his prosecution witnesses in chief. The evidence is given either on oath or by solemn affirmation. The purpose is to assist the witness to put forward his version of what he saw and what he did. The questions must not suggest the answer. This is called 'leading' the witness and can only be done if that part of the evidence is agreed, e.g. that the officer was on duty at a specific time and place, or in very specific circumstances.

Example:

'Is it correct that on at 6 p.m. on the 1st May, you saw a man with a tattoo on his right arm, strike John Smith, the victim in his face with a clenched fist?' **X**

Not allowed! This is a 'leading question'!

Instead - examination-in-chief:

- Where were you at 6 p.m. on the 1st May?
- What did you see?
- You say that you saw two men shouting at each other and one of them struck the other.
- Can you describe the man who struck the blow?
- Was there anything at all distinctive about his appearance?
- Would you describe how the blow was struck?
- What happened next?

- **Cross-examination**

This is followed by cross-examination by the 'other side', i.e. the prosecutor cross-examines the defence witnesses and vice versa. The purpose is to probe the version of events and check out the accuracy and truthfulness. Differences between the original statement and the evidence given in court often forms the basis of cross-examination e.g. 'Today you are saying that you were 3 feet away but in your statement you said you were 3 metres - quite a difference - which was it?' This applied particularly when witnesses could only take contemporaneous statements into the witness box. This changed in April 2004. There is now a presumption that a witness may refresh their memory from a statement made after the event, provided that he indicates that it was indeed his recollection at the time of making the statement and it was likely to be significantly better at that time.

Cross-examination may include leading questions, and questions which attempt to discredit the evidence, e.g. 'I put it to you that you are mistaken about what happened because you were too far away to see clearly - that is the reality isn't it?'

- **Re-examination and clarification**

The prosecutor may then re-examine on any new matters which have arisen or explain answers which have been given in cross-examination. Finally the magistrates may ask any clarifying questions and should safely begin with 'May we clarify …' in order to avoid raising any new matters.

All witnesses should be thanked for their attendance and the chairmen checks with the prosecution and defence whether they can safely be released or whether they should remain at the back of the court because they may need to be re-called. Very occasionally, witnesses may be re-called if unforeseen evidence emerges through the case. When witnesses are released, even over the lunch period, they should be warned not to discuss the case until it is concluded.

- **No case to answer**

Once the prosecution case is complete, the court may dismiss the case either on the submission of the defence or on its own initiative. The criteria for finding no case to answer at this stage are: -

- There is no evidence to prove an essential element in the alleged offence.

Example:

The offence of criminal damage requires proof that the defendant committed the act of damage, but it must also be proved that he intended or was reckless as to whether the damage was caused. Accidental damage is not a criminal offence. If there is no proof of intention or recklessness, there is no case to answer.

- The prosecution evidence is so manifestly unreliable or tenuous that it cannot be relied upon e.g. witnesses giving widely different versions of events, key witness discredited under cross-examination, insubstantial identification evidence.

The court must consider whether a reasonable tribunal could convict at this stage. The prosecution must be given the opportunity to respond before the decision is made, so that comment may be made on the significance of any omissions or contradictions.

- **Defence case**

The defendant is under no obligation to give evidence and he may choose to remain silent. However, he <u>must</u> be warned that if he does choose not to give evidence then the court may draw an 'inference from his silence' i.e. it may understandably come to the conclusion that he has something to hide.

The failure to give evidence cannot be the only factor to justify a conviction, and it is very important to stress in the reasons for the decision, the nature of other supporting evidence. However, the silence may properly <u>contribute</u> to the totality of evidence which proves beyond reasonable doubt that the defendant is guilty. The same inference applies if the defendant chooses not to answer questions during the course of his evidence. For example, in a case of being drunk and disorderly the defendant chooses not to answer a question asking how much alcohol he had to drink. Marginally better to respond with, 'I can't remember'! Again the court must give an appropriate warning.

Occasionally the prosecution case may include the 'evidence of silence' during the actual investigation. This may be a silence, when asked if he had anything to say at the time of arrest/charge; when asked why he happened to be at the scene of the crime; when asked why he had stolen property in his possession and blood on his sleeve. Account should be given as to whereabouts and evidence, otherwise inferences may be drawn from such silences in the same way.

The defendant normally gives evidence first, followed by his witnesses, following the same order of questioning as for the prosecution witnesses:

- Examination in chief by the party calling the witness i.e. the defence asking open questions.
- Cross examination by the other party, i.e. the prosecutor asking challenging questions.
- Re-examination by the defence - any new matters raised.
- Clarification by the bench - clarifying only!

- **Defence closing address**

The defendant is given the right to address the court at the end of the evidence and may summarise his case and draw out any particular points which have been given for and against his case. The prosecutor may reply on legal points only. The legal adviser gives any final advice in open court so that the advocates may comment upon it.

If the magistrates wish the legal adviser to join in the retiring room, they should make this indication clear in open court. Words on the lines of 'When we have made our decision we will ask our legal adviser to join us to record our reasons'. If advice on a point of law is sought, then this must be aired in open court for comment.

7.8.   Structured approach to verdict

See Adult Bench Book -1.35.

The decision-making following a trial will normally be conducted in the retiring room and the following process is based upon the structure recommended by the Judicial Studies Board, which provides a clear framework for recording and announcing reasons.

Verdict reasons – example

Charge of criminal damage.

A.   What has to be proved and by whom?

What are the elements of the offence charged?

There are 2 elements to the criminal damage charge - (i) that damage was caused by the defendant and (ii) that this was either intentional or reckless.

What is the burden of proof and where does it fall?

The prosecutor must prove the offence beyond reasonable doubt.

B.   Examine the evidence

Identify what facts are agreed

It is agreed that the defendant caused damage to the window valued at £200.

Identify what facts are disputed

It is disputed that it was an intentional kick or reckless kick. The defence say that it was caused by an accidental fall.

Exclude any evidence which is not admissible

We exclude the hearsay evidence given by one of the witnesses that her friend heard the defendant bragging about the incident.

Any inferences to be drawn from silence during the investigation or the trial?

We note that the defendant failed to account for the glass splinters inside his shoe when interviewed in the presence of his solicitor and he did not reply to the prosecutor's question "You did kick the window, didn't you?

The question was repeated. The legal adviser gave a warning about the implication of his silence. Again he failed to answer. We <u>add</u> this to the clear evidence given by the prosecution witnesses.

C. Is the case proved?

Preferred evidence

We find that the damage was caused by an intentional kick. The two prosecution witnesses gave consistent eye-witness evidence of a deliberate 'kung-fu' kick' and we find them to be reliable witnesses. The defendant gave a confused and improbable version of events that he tripped and fell backwards and damaged the window purely with his body weight. The defendant did not call any other witnesses.

Has the burden of proof been discharged in respect of all elements of the offence?

We find that the case is proved beyond reasonable doubt and we find you guilty of criminal damage.

Reasons should not normally take up more than half a side to a side of paper unless there are separate issues surrounding numerous witnesses or arguments in law to be determined. It is important to recognise that the Practice Direction 2000 states that 'it shall be the legal adviser's responsibility to assist the court, where appropriate, as to the formulation of reasons and the recording of those reasons'. Furthermore, the legal adviser has the responsibility to advise on 'the appropriate decision making structure to be applied in any given case', 'whether or not the justices have requested that advice'. Use the legal adviser!

Specific applications to the court

7.9. Search warrants

Whilst search warrants play a vital part in many criminal investigations, it should always be remembered that the court is effectively giving the police the right to break into someone's house possibly during the night if necessary. Although the list of enquiries appears to be lengthy, they are brief checks and brief questions which may occasionally prevent the possibility of lifetime trauma for innocent people. A warrant may be considered for anywhere in England or Wales. It is a discretionary decision and the application is dealt with in private by a single magistrate. Notes should always be taken.

Checking the applicant and the application

- Check officer's warrant card/identity and that the application has been authorised by an Inspector, or other senior officer if urgent.
- Check that the legal basis for the application is identified e.g. drugs (Misuse of Drugs Act 1971), stolen goods (s.26 Theft Act 1968).

- A written information is required and the applicant officer must be sworn or affirm.
- Check that the premises to be searched are clearly defined e.g. garage at rear of ...., flat number ...and identify the articles being sought e.g. heroin.

Legal requirements

The magistrate must have reasonable grounds for believing that:

- A serious arrestable offence has been committed.
- There is material on the premises, specified in the application, which is likely to be of substantial value to the investigation.
- The material is likely to be relevant and is not in an excluded/special procedure category.
- Entry will not be granted without a warrant, or the purpose of search may be frustrated or seriously prejudiced unless a constable arriving at the premises can secure immediate entry, or it is not practicable to communicate with any person entitled to grant entry/access to the premises.

Suggested questions to ask

The occupiers

- Who is the anticipated occupier of the property?
- What is known about him?
- Has he got any previous convictions?
- Is he currently the subject of criminal proceedings?
- Are there any young children or other vulnerable occupants?
- If so, what arrangements are in place to care for them during the search and in the event of arrests? e.g. officer to accompany for specific purpose and local social services office are informed.

The information source

- What is the nature of any police surveillance of the property?
- When was the information received?
- Is the informant registered?
- Has the informant previously been used and found to be reliable?
- If anonymous source, what steps have been taken to corroborate the information?

The area

- Is the area ethnically sensitive?
- If so, what steps have been taken to try and diffuse any problems? e.g. police to be accompanied by police community liaison officer.
- When is the warrant to be executed? If any delay is expected, why is this? If during the night, why is this necessary?

Before granting the warrant, the magistrate should have a picture of the property involved, the probable occupier and what is to be sought. Is it reasonable to issue a search warrant in all the circumstances? It is appropriate to ask whether a previous application has been made and refused. If so, there should be additional grounds for a second application.

On granting the application, the date and time of grant must be noted on the information and both the information and the warrant must be signed. The information is retained by the court and the police must forward the search warrant after one month at the latest, executed or not, endorsed as to whether the articles were found and whether any other articles were seized.

The police are a public authority and in terms of practical execution they also have responsibility for ensuring compliance with the Human Rights Act. Operational issues should be left to the police e.g. when to execute the warrant.

7.10. Utility warrants - gas and electricity - right to enter

Applications may be made for warrants of entry to premises for various purposes, for example for entry to read a meter or to cut off a power supply following non-payment of the bill. Gas and electricity supplies may be cut off where the customer has not paid following a demand in writing, and after notice of the intention to cut off the supply. This power is not available if there is a dispute as to the amount owed.

After appropriate notice, an officer of the supplier may at all reasonable times enter the property for the purpose of cutting off the supply. The right of entry may only be exercised with the consent of the occupier or by warrant.

The court may grant a warrant on sworn information in writing and the magistrate must be satisfied that:

- Notice of the application has been given to the occupier (right to fair trial).
- Admission is reasonably required for the specified purpose.
- The applicant has a statutory right of entry to the premises.
- The requirements of any enactment have been complied with e.g. a code of practice exists to avoid cutting off vulnerable people during the winter months if at all possible.
- That relevant notices have been given.

Premises must be left secure following entry and any damage must be made good.

EVIDENCE

7.11. Basic rules of evidence

Evidence is a specialised subject and is complex. It is most likely to be an issue during a trial and reasons must include any determinations which are made about any evidential issues. Evidence which is able to be considered by the court is referred to as 'admissible' and evidence which cannot be considered is referred to as 'inadmissible'. Sometimes statements are made in court which are 'inadmissible' and they must be struck out from any notes and disregarded.

Most 'rules' of evidence have exceptions to them in certain circumstances so it is always worth checking with the legal adviser. Subject to those exceptions, the <u>general</u> rules are as follows. N.B. virtually every one carries exceptions!

- The test for all evidence is that it is 'relevant'. It must either aim to prove or disprove some matter which requires to be proved.
- Criminal cases must be proved beyond reasonable doubt. That does not go so far as 'beyond a shadow of a doubt'. Civil cases must be proved on the balance of probabilities - 'being more likely than not'. The most notable exception being a civil application for an ASBO which must be proved beyond reasonable doubt.
- The burden of proving the case normally lies on the prosecutor in criminal cases and on the complainant in civil cases.
- Evidence is generally admissible if it relates to the facts in issue e.g. the quantity of alcohol in an offence of driving over the prescribed limit.
- Advocates cannot ask their own witness any 'leading' questions which suggest the answer e.g. Mr. Client, I put it to you that you were not present at the scene of the crime. That is correct isn't it?' The exception is when they are permitted by the other side to lead evidence which is agreed, e.g. where the witness was at the time, where the stolen vehicle was left by the owner etc.
- The magistrates may only ask questions which clarify issues already raised in a trial and new matters cannot be raised even if there has been a glaring omission by either of the advocates.
- Inferences may be drawn from silence in court and also from failing to answer particular questions from the point of charge and throughout the trial, but silence can never be the sole basis for a conviction.
- Identification evidence based on brief sightings must always be considered carefully. The court must consider the period of the sighting, whether the person was already known to the witness, the lighting, any special reason for remembering the accused, the period between observing and the subsequent identification to the police, and any material discrepancy between the description and the actual appearance. These are known as the 'Turnbull' guidelines.
- In criminal proceedings it is not generally admissible to prove the truth of the statement for someone to give evidence of something said by someone else. 'Someone else' is not available to cross-examine as to the truth of the statement. This is known as 'hearsay' evidence, e.g. 'Mrs. Smith told me that she saw the defendant steal it'. Similarly it is not generally admissible for a witness to give evidence as to a written statement made by someone else - they should really be in court to produce their statement. There are exceptions (see 7.12).

7.12. Hearsay evidence

If certain conditions apply then the Criminal Justice Act 2003 draws together the situations where a statement which is not made in oral evidence in the proceedings is admissible. The Act preserves the common law categories e.g. documents made by a public officer for the public such as registers; dictionaries, maps etc; confessions; admissions by the defendant's agent; and expert evidence.

The principal categories of hearsay which may be admitted are as follows:
- The parties agree that the hearsay may be admitted

- The witness is not available and one of the conditions below apply:
  - He is dead
  - He is unfit to attend because of his physical or mental condition
  - He is outside the UK and it is not reasonably practicable to secure his attendance
  - He cannot be found although such steps as it is reasonably practicable to take to find him have been taken
  - Through fear the person does not give, or continue to give oral evidence and the court gives leave for the statement to be given in evidence. The court must consider the contents of the statement, the risk of unfairness because of the inability to challenge the maker, and also whether special measures, e.g. use of screens, video link from October, would enable the witness to give oral evidence instead.

- Business, trade and other documents

Basically the document must be created or received in the course of the supplier's trade and he might reasonably have been supposed to have had personal knowledge of the matters. If it was passed through any other person, it was also in the course of their trade. Additionally one of the conditions above would apply, or, more usually, the person could not reasonably be expected to have any recollection of the matters e.g. due to the length of time since it was made. If the court is doubtful as to the statement's reliability, it may direct that it is not admissible.

- The court is satisfied that it is in the interests of justice

This is the open-ended option. The court must consider the probative value, other evidence on the matter, the circumstances under which it was made, and the apparent reliability of the maker of the statement. It must also consider the extent of the prejudice caused by not being able to challenge the statement, and of course, why oral evidence cannot be given.

The prosecutor must give notice of hearsay evidence along with the advance information. The defence may oppose the evidence going into court within 14 days, but the court may extend the period and allow oral application. Opposition is likeliest when a request is made in respect of a witness who is said to be too fearful to attend court.

7.13. Bad character

The Criminal Justice Act 2003 has made significant changes. Subject to a few specific exceptions, the general picture before December 2004, was that a defendant always presented at trial as someone of good character. It was only after a finding of guilt that previous convictions would be presented to determine the appropriate sentence. So far as witnesses were concerned, they previously faced the prospect of having their character attacked in the witness box. It is now possible, but by no means, usual, for the trial court to be made aware of misconduct and any previous convictions of the defendant, and the witness is now protected unless it is either agreed or the court specifically allow such evidence.

'Bad character' is defined as 'evidence of, or a disposition towards, misconduct on his part'. The section goes on to say that it 'has to do with the alleged facts of the offence charged, or is evidence of misconduct in connection with the investigation or prosecution of that offence' (s.98). 'Bad character' is not therefore confined to previous convictions. Inevitably they will be the clearest source of evidence of misconduct. It could extend for instance to evidence of police call outs where no charge actually followed, professional malpractice, marital misconduct, drug-taking, and evidence of misbehaviour which would fall short of a criminal offence.

7.13.1. 'Bad character' of a non-defendant, e.g. a witness

There are three situations where this can be admissible:

- The parties agree that the bad character may be admitted
- It is important explanatory evidence
- It has 'substantial probative value' relating to a matter which is in dispute and is also of 'substantial importance' to the case as a whole

Example:

The defendant is charged with assault. He asks for the victim's record of violence to be put before the court as it shows the victim's propensity to violence. It is relevant to the issue of why the defendant reacted as he did and his defence of self-defence. It may well help to explain that he really did have good grounds to believe that he was going to be assaulted himself - the victim is known as a violent man. The court may properly enquire about the circumstances of the convictions. Are they recent enough? Were the circumstances similar? If so, they would be likely to be admitted.

7.13.2. 'Bad character' of a defendant

There are seven 'gateways' to admissibility. The first five are of passing interest because the bad character evidence will simply appear before the trial court. The final two are more significant because they may be excluded by the court on application.

- The parties agree e.g. the defendant may wish to make it clear that he has always pleaded guilty in the past to a number of offences in order to demonstrate that this charge is an exception and he really is not guilty on this one.

- Evidence is given by the defendant himself or is given in answer to a question asked by him in cross-examination and he intended to elicit it e.g. defendant testifies about aspects of his misconduct such as drunkenness and drug-taking which affected his sense of judgement.
- It is important explanatory background evidence, e.g. the problematic relationship between the defendant and the victim.
- It has substantial value in relation to an important matter in issue between the defendant and a co-defendant e.g. blame is put on the co-defendant who already has a similar conviction.
- It is evidence to correct a false impression given by the defendant e.g. if he puts himself forward as a man of good character and he actually has a criminal record.

Subject to application to the court to exclude:

- Defendant has made an attack on another person's character, that he has committed an offence or behaved in a reprehensible way.
- Prosecution evidence where it is relevant to an important issue between the defendant and prosecution. (s.101).

7.13.3. Court power to exclude 'bad character' evidence

When the gateway relates to attack on another person's character or relates to an important issue between the defendant and prosecution, application may be made to the court to exclude the evidence. The scenario is normally that the defendant does not want previous convictions to be put before the trial court. It must not be admitted if the court considers that it would have such an adverse effect on the fairness of the proceedings that the court ought not to admit it, by weighing the probative value against the prejudicial effect.

The 'matters in issue' between the prosecution and defence include the question whether the defendant has a propensity to commit offences of the kind with which he is charged ...and/or be untruthful. This may be established by convictions for offences of the same description or category as the one with which he is charged. This gateway is the one which is the most commonly relied upon by the prosecution and the court is likely to be involved in applications by the defence to exclude previous convictions. The case below has helped enormously in guiding decisions as to what should and what should not be excluded.

7.13.4. Case law guidance on excluding bad character

R v. Nicky Hanson, March 2005, Court of Appeal.

This case sets out three helpful questions to consider

- Does the history of previous convictions establish a propensity to commit offences of the kind charged?

- Does that propensity make it more likely that the defendant committed the offence charged?
- Is it unjust to rely on the convictions of the same description or category and in any event, will the proceeding be unfair if they are admitted?

A single conviction will often not show propensity, e.g. a single shoplifting conviction, unless it is unusual, e.g. child sexual abuse, fire setting. Would a conviction for deception always create a propensity to untruthfulness? No. Only if there is an issue regarding truthfulness in the current offence or a jury has previously disbelieved the defendant and found him guilty in the past.

Evidence of bad character cannot be used to bolster a weak case or prejudice the bench against the defendant. Propensity is only one factor and must be assessed in the light of all the other evidence of the case.

The offences in the case were burglary and theft from dwelling. The record was considered. It was said that handling and aggravated taking without consent, although within the theft category, did not, without more pertinent information show a propensity to burgle or steal. The robbery, also within the theft category, might have been so prejudicial as to adversely affect the fairness of the proceedings. Burglary and theft from dwelling were properly admissible to show propensity to commit the offence of the kind charged.

In the case of R v. Pickstone, the offences were indecent assault on a child, and rape, before the court in January 2005. His record revealed an indecent assault on an 11 year old girl in 1993 when he was sentenced to a 2 year probation order. This was of the same description and category. So far as the passage of time was concerned the judge said ' a defendant's sexual mores and motivations are not necessarily affected by the passage of time' and the admission of the conviction was not unjust even though it was 'spent'. This case sets a clear precedent that sexual offences may be considered under the bad character provisions even though the rehabilitation period has long expired.

7.13.5. Procedure to introduce bad character evidence

Applications must be made on the relevant forms set out in the Practice Direction. If the prosecutor wishes to introduce evidence of a defendant's bad character he must give notice with the initial disclosure, and the defence application to exclude it must be received by the court office and all parties within 7 days of the notice. This enables the matter to be considered as a pre-court binding ruling well in advance of the court hearing. However, the court may allow the notice and application to be made orally and it may extend the time limit even if it has expired. A trial court could therefore be faced with determining the evidential issue before the trial begins if it allowed late oral notice to be given. This would require some very good reason for the delay, given the starting point for the time limits which will have expired a long time before the trial.

7.14 Special measures

Increasingly there is recognition that if there is no witness there is no justice. Being a witness is rarely a happy experience, and it is not surprising that witnesses are often reluctant to come forward and face the prospect of being cross-examined about their recollection of events. The court witness service provide valuable support on the day of the trial, and the police and CPS are working towards improved witness care from the time of the incident through the developing witness care units.

Legislation has also created 'special measures' to make the experience of giving evidence less daunting. These may be specifically applied for, or the court may raise the issue itself. The criteria for making a special measures direction is that it must be likely to maximise so far as practicable the quality of the evidence, taking account of the views of the witness and whether the measure would inhibit the evidence being effectively tested.

The following special measures are available in the Magistrates' Court. They apply in respect of children, and a child is deemed to be in need of special protection if the offence is sexual or violent. The provisions extend to vulnerable adults and those who are intimidated in October 2005. In all scenarios the bench, the legal representatives and any interpreter must be able to see and hear the witness and vice versa. Arrangements may need to be made to transfer a case to a court with the relevant facilities. The facilities are available for criminal cases and civil applications for ASBOs.

- Screening the witness from the accused
- Giving evidence by live link - evidence by a live television link or other arrangement whereby the witness is absent from the courtroom
- Giving evidence in the absence of specified persons - this does not include the accused who must remain in court and also a nominated member of the Press

Video recorded evidence in chief is available in respect of child witnesses who are in need of special protection e.g. the victim of a sexual offence, and this may be played to the court. The use of intermediaries is currently being piloted where it is considered necessary for someone to explain the questions put and to communicate the answers given.

A special measures direction may also be made in respect of aids to communication so that witnesses are provided with appropriate devices so that questions and answers may be effectively communicated e.g. some courts are equipped with hearing loop technology.

CHAPTER 8
SENTENCING

* Key: Sections in this chapter relate to the Criminal Justice Act 2003 and are quoted in respect of major changes. **'SGC'** refers to the published guidelines of the Sentencing Guidelines Council.

8.1. Structured approach to sentencing

The Criminal Justice Act brings a number of changes to the structured approach which are summarised in the checklist below, and then discussed in detail from 8.2. The sentencing structure can be summarised as the 4 'O's - Offence, Offender, Objectives and Options.

1. Offence

| **Normal sentence for offence(s) =** | (Sentencing Guideline entry point given as before) |

Culpability *(New - s.143(1))

• Intentional	
Check with your legal adviser if lesser level of culpability: • Reckless • Knowledge of the risk, even if did not intend to cause the harm • Negligent (*SGC)	

Harm *(New - s.143(1))

Actual harm caused	
Risk of harm – intended or might foreseeably have caused	

| Aggravating features of specific offence
e.g. Relevant previous convictions, high value | Mitigating features of specific offence |

2. Offender mitigation

3. Objectives/Purposes *(New - s.142(1)):

What purpose(s) does the court aim to achieve?

| Punishment | Reduction in crime/deterrence | Reform and rehabilitation | Protection of the public | Reparation |

3. Options Seriousness level =

Discharge, i.e. 'Inexpedient to punish' (as before)	
Fine (as before)	
'Serious enough' *(New - SGC) Breakdown of Community Order to high/medium/ low levels <u>and</u> 'Even if threshold is passed, a fine or discharge may be appropriate' (SGC).	High Medium Low Fine
So serious' *(New - s.152) Custody <u>only if</u> 'neither a fine alone nor a community penalty can be justified' Consider a fine (unlikely but possible); Community Order (High level) 'where the custody threshold is crossed but a community sentence is more appropriate' (SGC); Custody; Suspended Sentence; Intermittent custody - (pilot areas only).	

Extent of credit for guilty plea *(New - specific guidance - SGC) =

| **Final sentence:** |

8.2. Offence - Culpability and Harm

These are two considerations which are now mandatory (s.143). The Sentencing Guidelines Council (SGC) has gone on to define the various levels of offender culpability as:

- Intentional with the highest culpability when an offence is planned. Many offences require intention in order to be made out. For example, theft must be intentional - there is no such thing as reckless or negligent theft.
- Reckless. For example, criminal damage may be committed either intentionally or recklessly, and the latter is less culpable and therefore less serious.
- Knowing of the risk even though he does not intend to cause the harm. This is a rare situation. Perhaps the scenario of the driver who drinks a high amount of alcohol and sensibly does not drive home at the time, but is aware of the slight possibility that he could still be over the limit on the following morning when he does drive.
- Negligent e.g. careless driving.

If culpability is determined at a level below 'intentional' it is worth checking with the legal adviser that the offence concerned is actually still made out.

The SGC give a list of factors indicating higher culpability and they include all the usual aggravating features with which we are familiar, e.g. offending on bail, abuse of trust, high profit etc.

The court must also consider 'any harm which the offence caused, was intended to cause or might foreseeably have caused'. Harm may take the form of physical injury, financial loss or psychological distress to an individual. It may also be harm to the community at large. The SGC list of factors indicating greater harm include the familiar factors such as offending against vulnerable victims, in the presence of children, sustained attacks and high value goods (including sentimental value).

Example:

An offence of criminal *damage* to a window valued at £100. Entry point is a band C fine.

- Defendant A is entertaining his friends, flailing his arms around and holding a bottle. He is shocked to realise that he has smashed the window.
  Culpability = Reckless. Harm = £100 damage to the window.
  Likely outcome - Fine + Compensation £100 (damage).
- Defendant B threw a brick through the window whilst the occupant stood inside the room.
  Culpability = Intentional. Harm = £100 damage to the window and also the foreseeable physical and psychological harm to the occupant.
  Likely outcome - aggravation to a Community Order + Compensation of £100 (damage) + £x (terror and distress).

8.2.1. Aggravating and mitigating features of offence

There are three statutory aggravating features which apply to every offence. Firstly, if an offence was committed whilst on bail, the court 'must treat the fact that it was committed in those circumstances as an aggravating factor'. It does not matter whether it is the same type of offence or not and it does not matter whether the bailed offence is ultimately discharged. Secondly, if an offence is racially or religiously aggravated (other than those specifically charged as such), again, the court 'must treat the fact as an aggravating factor'.

Thirdly an offence must be aggravated if the offender was motivated or demonstrated hostility based on sexual orientation or disability of the victim (New.s.146).

Other aggravating and mitigating features are specific to the offence itself and the most common specific features are listed in the Magistrates Court Sentencing Guidelines.

Example: Theft

Sentencing Guideline entry point (p.60) = Community penalty

Aggravating features - High value; Planned; Sophisticated; Adult involving children; Organised team; Related damage; Vulnerable victim.
Mitigating features - Low value; Impulsive actions.

8.2.2. Previous convictions

The court must treat a previous conviction as an aggravating feature if it is reasonable to do so, having regard to the nature of the offence and its relevance to the current offence, and also the time which has elapsed (143(2)).

The nature and relevance rests broadly on whether the offence falls within the same category - offences against the person (violence and disorder), offences against property (theft, damage etc.) or traffic offences. An offence of theft cannot reasonably be said to aggravate an offence of assault - they are entirely dissimilar. So far as elapse of time is concerned, the statutory rehabilitation provisions do not apply to criminal proceedings, and during the course of debate in parliament it was specifically said that 'convictions' would include 'spent' convictions. That said, the court may have regard to the rehabilitation provisions. For instance, a 5 year gap of offending is required after the imposition of a community sentence or a fine, and a 10 year gap is required after the imposition of a 6 months to 30 months custodial sentence before it is considered 'spent' under the provisions.

The record is also significant in that it discloses the previous penalties and the response in terms of whether or not further offending occurred is relevant to both level of culpability and also choice of sentence (SGC). The sentence even for a dissimilar offence is therefore relevant in making that choice.

8.3. Offender personal mitigation

This includes age, especially youth, and mental and physical health. The issue of co-operation with the police must not be overlooked in computing sentence. The defendant who gives a false name and address initially, even following a minor traffic offence, causes an enormous amount of additional time and effort, and is an attempt (sometimes successful) to avoid prosecution.

Other aspects of offender mitigation set out in case law are:

- Positive good character e.g. no relevant previous convictions, solid employment record, faithful discharge of family duties.
- Hard evidence of genuine remorse e.g. apology to the victim. This is a step further than the solicitor simply saying that his client is very sorry.
- If the offence is fuelled by drink or drugs – a genuine self-motivated determination to address the addiction. Again, this is rather more than a general expression of future intention.
- Youth/immaturity would often justify a less rigorous penalty than for an adult.
(R v Howells 1998).

The court may feel that further information is required and the services of the probation service may be called upon at this stage. The nature of the involvement will depend upon the information required and the sentence(s) which the court has in mind.

8.4. Objectives/Purposes

The court must now 'have regard' to the purpose(s) of the sentence to be imposed and they are listed below (s.142). What sentencing objectives or purposes are necessary and/or likely to be most effective? At this stage, it may well emerge that there are one or more purposes and therefore, one or more, penalties are necessary. Each purpose may be achieved potentially by a range of penalties.

- Punishment - where basic 'pay-back' to the community is required to emphasise that rules exist and must be kept and crime does not pay, e.g. fine, compensation, unpaid work, punitive curfew to restrict liberty.
- Protection of the public - where a penalty is required to create a greater protection for the specific victim or the community, from this defendant, e.g. custody, curfew during hours of offending, anti-social behaviour order, binding over order, licensed premises exclusion order, football banning order, restraining order. Many of the associated penalties for protection of the public rely heavily on being imposed on the bench's initiative, e.g. bolt-on ASBO with requirements to keep away from the victim and the offending area.
- Reform and rehabilitation - where there is realistic optimism for a positive change of behaviour e.g. a community order, with supervision and accredited programme requirements.
- Reparation - compensation to the victim: unpaid work.
- Reduction in crime/deterrence to others - in the occasional situation where it is necessary to deter particular types of offending and it is essential for the safety of the community, that the court send out a clear message that custody can be expected, e.g. local riots.

8.5. Options

- What is the level of seriousness? Is the offence 'serious enough' or 'so serious', or 'too serious' (committal for sentence)?
- What is the most suitable option to satisfy identified sentencing purpose(s)?
- Is a standard pre-sentence report required, or a fast-track report as a stand-down from the list?

8.5.1. Credit for guilty plea

The court must take into account the stage in the proceedings at which the offender indicated his intention to plea guilty and the circumstances in which this indication was given. If, as a result the court imposes a punishment which is less severe, it shall state in open court that it has done so (s.152))

A guilty plea avoids the need for a trial, shortens the gap between charge and sentence, saves considerable cost and saves witnesses from the concern about having to give evidence. It is entirely separate to aggravation and mitigation, admissions to the police and matters to be taken into consideration, which determine the length of sentence before reduction (SGC). The reduction applies to punitive elements, e.g. fine, unpaid work, curfew. It does not apply to other elements, e.g. supervision and accredited programmes which are determined by the seriousness level and the needs of the defendant. Nor does credit apply to ancillary orders, e.g. disqualification.

The SGC (Sentencing Guidelines Council) recommend a sliding scale reduction as follows, based upon when the guilty plea is entered:

- First reasonable opportunity = maximum of 1/3
- After the trial date is set = maximum of 1/4
- At the door of the court/after the trial has begun = maximum of 1/10
- After trial = no reduction

It is now clarified by the SGC that there is no reason why credit should be reduced if the offender is caught 'red-handed'. It should be made clear to the defendant what the benefit has been of pleading guilty - he has co-operated and avoided the need for a trial. It should be made clear that this is the reason why the sentence has been reduced. Simply saying 'we have given you credit for pleading guilty' does not automatically imply a reduction in sentence to many defendants. There is a strong suspicion that the 'word is not out' in all quarters that it is good to plead guilty quickly, particularly in the youth court.

In straightforward cases the reduction may even be specified e.g. Unpaid hours requirement is reduced by 1/3 from 60 hours to 40 hours.

8.5.2. Proportionate and commensurate

The totality of the final penalty must be 'commensurate with seriousness' and the restriction on the individual must be 'proportionate' to the offence. Some pruning may be necessary!

Examples:

- A perfectly calculated fine on several offences based properly on net income and band may well result in a total which will take well over 12 months to pay. Overall, the fine needs to be reduced.

- A cocktail of options may perfectly cover the necessary purposes of rehabilitation and protection - supervision, accredited programme and curfew. This is a heavy restriction - maybe too heavy, and all elements may need to be reduced in quantity so that overall it is proportionate to the offence, e.g. curfew reduced to only 2 months for weekends only.

8.5.3. Offences taken into consideration ('TICs')

The totality must also reflect offences which the defendant has asked to be taken into consideration. These are offences which an offender admits, usually in a police interview, and he can then formally ask the court for offences to be 'taken into consideration' at sentence. The defendant avoids the risk of further prosecution at a later stage; the victims may receive compensation even though the offence is not charged, and the court has the benefit of a full picture of offending. The offences to be taken into consideration must be similar to the charged offence and there must be sufficient evidence of the offence for it to potentially stand as a separate charge. The magistrates will be made aware of the schedule of the offences which are admitted e.g. 10 similar matters of obtaining property with a stolen credit card, which will increase the penalty for the two charged offences of theft of the card and obtaining property by deception.

8.6. Sentencing reasons

Giving reasons for sentence is a human right. Article 6 requires judgement to be pronounced 'publicly' and Convention case law is clear that the giving of reasons is a part of the right to a fair trial, with two main purposes: -

- To ensure that justice is done, and is seen to be done by the person to whom the decision is addressed, and by the community at large.
- To enable an aggrieved party to consider whether to exercise his right of appeal against the decision.

Purely and simply, it shows 'where the decision came from'. It is not expected be a House of Lords judgement – just a few meaningful comments.

The structured approach ensures that the key reasons will emerge. In some cases, there will be little to consider or say if the normal entry point is used and there is basically nothing to increase or reduce the sentence. In other cases, there will be far more to consider in weighing aggravation and mitigation, particularly where the end result is to move out of the guideline entry point. The example below uses the structured approach as described above:

1. Offence - culpability, harm and aggravation/mitigation
2. Offender mitigation
3. Objectives/purposes to be achieved
4. Options - determining level of seriousness and giving credit for guilty plea.

Sentencing reasons - example

Criminal damage

1. **Offence**
   We are dealing with an offence of criminal damage, *and*
   The normal guideline sentence would be a fine, *but*

In your case the offence was intentional because you took a brick to throw through the window.

The damage was £100 for the broken window and the distress caused to Miss Smith as she avoided the breaking glass as the window broke.

The offence is made more serious by the fact that you were on bail at the time, and have convictions in the past year for similar offences of disorderly behaviour and assault.

2. Offender
In your favour you have completed your community punishment order and you are now in full time employment.

3. Objectives/purposes
We feel that you need some help to stop offending and we need to compensate and protect Miss. Smith.

4. Options
In all the circumstances the offence is serious enough for us to make a community order.

This will include two requirements of supervision for 12 months and a curfew for 4 months from 7 p.m. to 6 a.m. You will also pay compensation of £100 for the broken window, and £100 for the terror and distress you caused to Miss Smith.

Credit for guilty plea
We have reduced the period of the curfew requirement by 2 months. This is because you have co-operated with the court to deal with this case as quickly as possible and avoided the need for her to come to court for a trial. It is therefore only 4 months instead of 6 months.

8.7. Sentencing options

Sentencing powers are built on a hierarchy of seriousness with an increasing restriction on liberty as set out in the table below.

Increase of seriousness and restriction of liberty →					
Inexpedient to punish	Fine	'Serious enough'	'So serious'	Too serious
Absolute Discharge Conditional Discharge (up to 3 years)	Fine Compensation (Possibly alone as 1st priority of a monetary penalty)	Offences on/after 4.4.05: Community Order with Requirements (up to 3 years) Fine	Custody Suspended Sentence (contd. overleaf)	Commit to Crown Court (more than 6 months for one offence)

		Offences → 4.4.05 Attendance Centre Order Community Rehabilitation Order Community Punishment Order Curfew Order Drug Treatment and Testing Order Deferred sentence	Intermittent Custody High community order Deferred sentence Fine (rare)	
Ancillary orders which may be added to final penalty: Disqualification (also available as a separate penalty for all offences) Anti-Social Behaviour Order Binding over order Compensation Costs Endorsement Exclusion from licensed premises Forfeiture Football banning order Parenting order Restraining order Sexual Offences Prevention Order Driving test/re-test - disqualified unless complies with provisional licence					

8.8. Discharge - Absolute and Conditional

The court must be of the opinion that 'it is inexpedient to inflict punishment'. When is it 'inexpedient' to punish to the extent of a full 'absolute discharge'? For instance, where a conviction is sought, possibly as a basis for compensation in the County/High Court, but there is extremely strong mitigation. Or a defendant may already be sentenced on other offences and it is either inappropriate or impractical to impose any additional penalty e.g. defendant is serving a lengthy custodial sentence and could not comply with any other penalty.

A conditional discharge is more common. The court considers that there must be a condition that no further offences are committed during a fixed period of up to the three years if the offence is go unpunished. If a further offence is committed within the specified period, e.g. 12 months, then the court may sentence for the original offence in addition to the new matter, e.g. a fine for the new offence and an additional fine for the original offence.

The discharge recognises that the offence is of a minor nature as it can properly go unpunished for evermore. There is a real belief that there will be no further offending and no actions need to be put in place to ensure that this happens. Conditional discharges are often urged as an appropriate outcome by the defence in domestic violence cases. The stage of considering purpose of sentence needs to be considered carefully. A discharge will seldom satisfy the usual purposes in such cases of rehabilitation and/or protection - a community order with an accredited programme may be more appropriate.

- ❑ Breach of the order = court may punish for the original offence.
- ⏱ No minimum. Maximum = 3 years.

8.9. Fines

'The amount of any fine fixed by a court shall be such as, in the opinion of the court, reflects the 'seriousness of the offence' and the guidelines give entry point bands for this purpose. 'In fixing the amount of any fine to be imposed on an offender, a court shall take into account the circumstances of the case including, among other things, the financial circumstances of the offender so far as they are known, or appear to the court.' The individual's net income is key to the calculation. There is no minimum figure. The maximum depends upon the amount fixed by law for the particular offence. The maximum fines are described as 'levels 1 to 5' rather than fixing specific amounts in every piece of legislation. This enables the various levels to be adjusted from time to time. As at October 2005, the levels are as follows:-

Level 1 = £200
Level 2 = £500 e.g. failing to send a statement of means to court on request
Level 3 = £1,000 e.g. disorderly behaviour
Level 4 = £2,500 e.g. racially or religiously aggravated disorderly behaviour
Level 5 = £5,000 e.g. no insurance, driving with excess alcohol.

A very small number of offences carry higher maxima e.g. some health and safety offences.

In practical terms, the amount of the fine is fixed after considering five aspects which are each considered below. They are the sentencing guideline band - net income calculation - aggravating/mitigating features - credit for guilty plea - effective order to pay.

8.9.1. Sentencing guideline band

All offences which have an entry point of 'fine' in the sentencing guidelines are given an entry band as follows:

Band A = 50% of net income e.g. drunk and disorderly
Band B = 100% of net income e.g. no insurance
Band C = 150% of net income e.g. criminal damage

This ensures a starting point figure which is individual to each defendant – not a range, but an actual figure for the individual. 'Ballpark' figures for particular offences are long gone. Two defendants convicted of no insurance with very different net incomes should leave court with very different fines.

8.9.2. Net income

This will normally be gleaned either from a completed means form or directly from the defendant in court. Debate continues after the introduction of the Guidelines as to what fairly constitutes the 'net income', which is described as 'weekly take home pay or benefit'. Whilst it is no doubt agreed that income tax and national insurance should be properly deducted before arriving at the net income, there are other aspects. Arguably, child benefit should be ignored as this is specifically allocated to the children and this ensures a higher protected income for a family.

A more complex aspect is the comparison between a defendant in receipt of benefits with no rent/mortgage or council tax to pay out of that income, as compared to a waged defendant who has roof costs and council tax to pay out of his income. Some benches have therefore taken the view that roof costs and council tax should be deducted from a waged income so that the 'net figure' is then fairly equated with that of the defendant on benefits i.e. both are fined from 'the money left to actually live on'. A defendant paying board – deduction of ½ as his notional roof cost contribution.

Example.

Defendant A is working and after tax/insurance, he receives £150 per week. Defendant B is in receipt of job-seekers allowance and receives £150 benefits.

Defendant A		*Defendant B*	
Take home pay (after tax/insurance)	= £150	Job seekers allowance	= £150
Less: Rent Council tax	= £40 = £10	Rent and council tax are covered by the state	= £0
Money for ordinary living expenses Net income = £100	= £100	Money for ordinary living expenses Net income = £150	= £150

This is a relatively straightforward calculation and ensures that the fine is fixed on the 'money in pocket' for food/clothes/entertainment for each defendant, and the 'roof costs' which cause substantial differences between those who pay and those who do not, are taken out of the calculation. Additionally the defendant on state benefits will normally have the privilege of other monetary passport benefits e.g. free school meals, community care grants, whilst the working defendant will have the expense of travelling to work, but these modifications would be too complex to work through. Rent/mortgage and council tax are the big ones!

Obviously it is relevant as to whether the defendant is solely responsible for paying out expenses, and to that extent only, the existence of a partner's income is relevant. The question is 'How much do you personally pay towards rent/mortgage/bills? rather than 'How much is the rent etc.?'

There is now a standard means form, and it an offence to fail to send details of means to the court if not attending, or to provide means information in court if the defendant attends. In practical terms the failure to supply is dealt with by making 'such determination as the court thinks fit' in the absence of the defendant. There are local variations in approaching this determination.

In West Yorkshire the figure is based upon an assumption that a defendant is in receipt of the local average net income and deducts the average rent/mortgage and council tax figures. These are readily accessible using the New Earnings survey/ Regional Trends and local authority figures. In West Yorkshire the relevant figures in 2000 gave £270 per week net income across both genders as an average across the various divisions, with an average rent/mortgage of £45pw and council tax of £5 (rounded down). This creates a fine in absence of £220 (£270 less rent/council tax). The fine for a 100% band B offence, e.g. no insurance is therefore £220, and for a 50% band A offence, e.g. no television licence, it is £110. The fine can later be rectified to the correct amount based on actual net income as and if the court becomes aware of the details - usually in subsequent fine default proceedings!

If the defendant does attend it may be necessary for the court to work through the details in open court - even when the form is completed there are often additional questions. If he refuses to do so, then the court may reasonably warn that they will fine the maximum for the offence with credit for guilty plea deducted, e.g. £5,000 for no insurance less 1/3 credit. The alternative is for the Crown Prosecutor to commence prosecution for the failure to supply means information.

8.9.3. Aggravating/mitigating circumstances

Using a structured approach, the aggravating and mitigating features of the offence must be considered, followed by offender mitigation, when considering quantum. If any of these factors come into play, then they should be announced in the reasons as explanation for deviation from the guideline figures. In many situations, particularly traffic document offences dealt with in the absence of the defendant, there will be no information before the court apart from the fact that documents were not produced. In those circumstances it will be difficult to justify an increase or decrease from the guideline.

It cannot be emphasised enough that deviation may well be perfectly appropriate, provided there is a clear reason which a reasonable person could understand.

Example: Drunk and disorderly - entry point - Band A, i.e. half net income.

Aggravating features: Abusive language to fellow passengers on a public bus. Had to be ejected by the driver; police assistance had to be sought, and the bus was delayed. Protracted incident with inconvenience and discomfort to others.

Fine increased to full income - Band B. (Bind over may also be appropriate).

8.9.4. Credit for guilty plea

A deduction of up to one third should normally be deducted for a timely guilty plea, e.g. a net income of £60 for a band B offence would carry an entry point fine of £40.

An easy reference fines calculator is available at Appendix B. This gives net weekly/monthly/annual incomes for each band together with the one third credit starting point figure. Remember this is a starting point only and can quite properly go up and down, but should ensure that a defendant will be fined roughly the same amount in any court for a standard offence.

8.9.5. Outgoings and limitation of the 12 month rule

Case law and the Sentencing Guidelines are clear that fines should normally be payable within a 12 month maximum period. The logic is that a fine penalty lies below the ultimate restriction on liberty of custody which can only be imposed for up to 12 months. The reality is that this is also the intensive input period for community orders also. It would be disproportionate for the 'lesser offender' to be penalised for longer, with the very real threat of custody for non-compliance throughout that period.

Outgoings are therefore relevant to check just how much can realistically be paid within 12 months if instalments are necessary. If the appropriate instalment rate is £5 per week, then effectively the maximum fine is £5 x 50 weeks = £250. This final aspect of fixing the fine can result in re-visiting the guideline fines for a multiple offender so that the total fine is reduced within the guideline period.

8.9.6. Order to pay

- The whole amount is due immediately and the first question must be 'Can it be paid in full now?' possibly by credit card.
- If not, 'How much can be paid now? There is the positive psychological commitment of 'paying a deposit' and the practical experience of getting things moving.
- If not, 'How quickly can it be paid? It is far easier to enforce a single payment within 14 days than instalment options if they are not really necessary.

- What is a fair and realistic instalment rate? This should have been considered when checking the 12 month capability. Warn the defendant that missed payments render the whole amount due immediately and default may result in imprisonment.
- The defendant may consent to the court applying for direct deduction from Job Seekers Allowance or Income Support - currently £5 per week (October 2005), or for an attachment of earnings order with deductions fixed at a national percentage rate. Note that the court is only applying for the deduction and not making the order to deduct! Some applications are unsuccessful and the defendant will then be notified and asked to pay himself.

8.9.7. Enforcement of fines

- **Administrative action**

It is important to recognise that steps are taken before court action in order to secure payment. This usually begins with a reminder letter which will be sent 14 days after the payment date or after 2 missed instalments. Discussion by telephone conversation or administrative hearings may result in officers with delegated powers extending the payment period or varying the amount of instalments at this stage. They cannot vary the total amount of the imposition - only the court may do this. When dealing with a defaulter it is worth asking 'What did you do when you got the reminder letter?' rather than 'Did you get the reminder letter?'

The next stage is likely to be the issue of a distress warrant, or a summons or warrant to attend default court. The means enquiry is aimed at establishing why payment has not been made as ordered, identifying the current financial situation using the standard means form and determining the most productive disposal. The first stage is to ensure that the correct figure is enforced.

- **'Getting the bill right' - remission, rectification, review and 1 day detention**

❏ **Remission**

The court may remit the whole or any part of a fine it thinks 'just' to do so. The court must 'have regard to a change of circumstances'. For example, if the net weekly income has decreased from £200 per week wage at imposition to £60 per week benefits, a band B fine would be remitted from £200 to £60. Remission may also be appropriate if it subsequently transpires that the defendant has acquired multiple outstanding fines (often in absence), so that a global figure is fixed which can be paid in around 12 months.

❏ **Rectification**

Where a defendant has been convicted in absence or, has otherwise failed to co-operate with the court in respect of providing means information, the court 'may make such determination as it thinks 'fit'. In West Yorkshire, fines in absence are determined on the basis of the average county net income figure of £220 per week in the absence of any other information.

If, on subsequently inquiring into means at a means enquiry, the court determines that it would have fixed a smaller amount or would not have fined the defendant at all, then it may remit the whole or part of the fine. This type of remission effectively 'rectifies' the fine.

- [ ] **One day detention**

It is not possible to 'remit' costs, excise penalties, or Crown Court fines (except with the consent of the Crown Court), but the situation may well be that the amounts simply cannot be paid in the circumstances. Costs alone may be written off with the consent of the person to whom they are payable. However, the use of one day detention (possibly with immediate release) as a notional or small final outcome is often required to 'clear the books' in such cases in 'the interests of justice.' It may also be used where there is no realistic enforcement method but equally there is no question of culpable neglect. It may be served either in court or in a police station until 8pm at the latest.

Distinguish from the order of overnight detention until 8 a.m. the following day with earlier release to enable the defendant to attend work. This is rarely used.

All options below must be considered, and reasons must be given as to why they are not appropriate before committing a defaulter to prison for non-payment.

- **Attachment of benefits and Attachment of earnings**

Whilst attachments may be applied for at imposition by consent, this is the first option for the court to consider at default, without consent. Application by the court for attachment is now obligatory by statute if the following circumstances exist:
- [ ] Payment is not made immediately
- [ ] The defendant is an existing defaulter
- [ ] The default cannot be disregarded e.g. it is not simply a single missed payment with an acceptable excuse during an otherwise good payment record
- [ ] It is not impracticable or inappropriate to make the order.

Examples of 'impracticable or inappropriate':

Attachment of earnings - self-employed; temporary employment; employment is at risk; already has 2 attachment of earnings orders; net earnings are less than £55 per week/£220 per month.

Attachment of benefits - not in receipt of the qualifying benefits namely income support, job seeker's allowance or pension credit, or already has the maximum of 3 debt deductions.

The deduction rate is not fixed by the court. The deduction rate for benefits is currently fixed at £5 per week (October 2005). The rate for earnings is fixed by a table of national periodic deductions, e.g. wages between £165 and £260 per week are deducted at the rate of 12%; between £260 and £370 per week are deducted at the rate of 17%.

Full payment details must be obtained e.g. pay number, insurance number, so that the application can be processed quickly by the Department of Work and Pensions (DWP) or employer. The defaulter will be notified whether the application has been successful, and if not, he must either pay himself, or he will be summoned back to court for another option to be considered.

- **Distress warrant**

The warrant authorises entry and removal by the bailiffs of money and goods to the value of the financial penalty + the bailiff's costs. The court must be satisfied that there are likely to be distrainable goods e.g. the defaulter admits that he is the sole owner of a car, or has a substantial income (a useful option if attachment of earnings is not practical). It may be issued forthwith, but in default proceedings it is more likely to be postponed, e.g. distress warrant postponed upon payment of £50 per calendar month so that there is a genuine opportunity to pay the fine without issuing the warrant. The defaulter must be given the opportunity to make representations.

The bailiffs may only enter property lawfully and they cannot break into property. They may not take clothes, bedding or tools of trade of the defaulter or his family. Six days must pass before any goods are sold and household goods must not be removed until the day of sale. It is an offence for the defaulter to remove or sell goods which have been distrained upon.

It may well be appropriate for the court to encourage payment by standing order to the court at this stage. The postponed distress warrant is the enforcement method if the payment is not made as ordered.

- **Money Payment Supervision Order (MPSO)**

A supervisor is specifically appointed e.g. a court enforcement officer or named probation officer. His duty is to 'advise and befriend the defendant with a view to inducing him/her to pay the sum adjudged to be paid and thereby avoid committal to custody, and to give any information required about conduct and means'. A report must be obtained before committal which will briefly outline the efforts to encourage payment and any response.

This option may be appropriate in situations when attachment is not possible and there are problems in organising finances or family responsibilities, and it must be specifically considered for defaulters under 21.

- **High Court/County Court action**

Alternative actions are open, in limited circumstances:

☐ Attachment of debts and garnishee proceedings - when a defaulter's own debtors are ordered to pay debts direct to the court if the debts have already been proved. This arises in the situation where a defaulter says that he would pay 'if only his cash-flow was sorted out and he was

paid all that he was owed'. Basically the court can join in to take the monetary orders straight from his debtors.
- ❏ Charging order - this imposes a charge on land or on an interest in land of the defaulter, or on his securities if the property is owned absolutely. For example, he owns his house solely and outright but will not pay the £1000 compensation – a charge for the £1000 can be imposed on the house.
- ❏ Appointment of a receiver for land or rent and profits - when a defaulter is a landlord whose income is essentially rent. The court cannot make an attachment of earnings but this is the second best option – to appoint a receiver for the rents and hand them to the court. It is important to check that there are no 3rd party rights to the rent.

In all three situations the court must consider the potential expense of taking the action and the prospects of recovery of the sum due. A distress warrant should always be tried first.

- **Attendance Centre Order**

The court may order a person under 25 to attend an attendance centre for a minimum of 12 hours and a maximum of 24 hours (to 18 years) and 36 hours (to 25 years), in default of paying a financial penalty. The defaulter must be present when the order is made and culpable neglect/wilful refusal must be found. All other options should therefore be considered first. The centre must be available locally and be reasonably accessible. Part payment will reduce the hours pro-rata. Breach of the order may result in custody/detention.

- **Committal to prison**

The following criteria apply:

- ❏ The defaulter must be present and a means enquiry must be held.
- ❏ Wilful refusal or culpable neglect must be found. Wilful refusal means a deliberate refusal to pay. Culpable neglect means a reckless disregard.
- ❏ The court must consider or try all other methods of enforcing payment and it must appear to the court that they are inappropriate or unsuccessful.
- ❏ The court must be of the opinion that no other method of dealing with the defaulter is appropriate.
- ❏ Legal representation must be offered and the court records must be disclosed to the defaulter if sought, with proper facility for the preparation of the defence.
- ❏ Reasons must be given, verbally in court, and in writing, for discarding all non-custodial options in respect of all defaulters.

* The above restrictions do not apply if the defaulter is already serving a custodial sentence.

Imprisonment may be imposed forthwith on the following scale: To £200 = 7 days; £201 to £500 = 14 days; £501 to £1,000 = 28 days; £1001 to £2,500 = 45 days. If part payments are made then the period is reduced proportionately. As with any other maximum period, the court must consider proportionality and a fair period must be fixed for the individual defendant, the seriousness of the default and the type of offences concerned. For instance, a series of parking offences could result in a lengthier period in default than a single serious offence. Imposition of a prison sentence in default should go beyond the simple equation of amount(s) and maximum period(s).

"The purpose of all enforcement measures is to compel payment and commitment to prison is no exception. If a defaulter actually serves a period of imprisonment, enforcement in his case has failed." (Lord Chancellors Division Best Practice Guide 1992).

- **Suspended committal**

Normally the period of custody will be suspended on payment being made if the court 'thinks expedient to do so', e.g. pay £10 per week or serve 7 days imprisonment in default.

The terms may subsequently be varied and the commitment may be further postponed if circumstances change. The defaulter must be notified in writing of the date and time if the court is considering the issue of the commitment following missed payments so that he may attend and make representations.

When the defaulter fails to respond to the notice, the commitment may be issued in the absence of the defaulter and he may be arrested and taken straight to prison unless the full amount is paid. The majority of defaulters do not attend court on notice that the commitment falls to be issued. A suspended committal may therefore result in arrest from home to prison, so it is important to stress from the point of imposition that custody really can be imposed on non-payment.

- **Future developments in fine enforcement - Collection Orders and Officers**

Following on from existing pilots, the roll out of the following provisions is expected to be complete by March 2006. The intention is to begin the enforcement process at imposition and proceed as far as possible on an administrative basis. A 'Collection Order' will be made in respect of every fine/compensation/costs imposition and previous orders will normally be consolidated. Administrative 'Fines Collection Officers' will be designated with the powers to:

- Vary the terms
- Apply for attachment of benefits/earnings
- Bring 'reserve terms', set by a magistrate, into force and vary if necessary, if an attachment is unsuccessful
- Clamp the offender's car (court permission will be required if a sale is necessary)
- Register the fine with the Register of Fines and Judgements, which may affect the defaulter's ability to obtain credit
- Issue a distress warrant
- Transfer the case to the civil courts for enforcement
- Refer the case to court.

The court will deal with any appeals from the sanction(s) used by the Fines Collection Officer, and may impose any alternative. In addition to existing court powers, it will be possible for the court to impose 'Fines payment work' which will be available if there is insufficient means - currently anticipated at the rate of £6 per hour (September 2005). The court may also increase the fine element by 50%, or, impose imprisonment.

8.10. Compensation

Compensation 'wears two hats' - as a sentence in its own right, or ancillary to another penalty, e.g. in addition to a Community Order. It relates to any personal injury, loss or damage, occasioned by an offence. 'Injury' includes 'terror and distress' e.g. to a frightened victim in the house when a window is smashed.

The amount is such as the court considers 'appropriate' having regard to any evidence, including victim personal statements, and to any representations made on behalf of the parties, up to a maximum of £5000. The Sentencing Guidelines set out guideline figures for injuries (page 90) e.g. £125 for a black eye. The Criminal Injuries Compensation Board does not make awards in a sum less than £1000. It is therefore important for the court to explore the possibility of compensation for such personal injuries e.g. loss of non-front tooth falls within range of £500 to £1000.

When there is a challenge and real issues are raised, evidence must be received, and complex/substantial matters should be left to the County Court. Reasons must be given if compensation is not granted in full e.g. insufficient evidence of loss, insufficient means to pay in full.

The maximum payment period is dependant upon means and can properly extend to 2 years or exceptionally 3 years - longer than the 12 month limitation on fines.

8.10.1. Enforcement of compensation

The enforcement options apply as for fines with two differences. Firstly, the Magistrates' Court is only saying that it is not going to enforce any further when custody or discharge is ordered. The compensation may still be enforced in the County Court High Court - it is not written off once and for all as fines are. Secondly, the court does not 'remit' if circumstances change, it adjourns for a 'review' with the potential of 'discharging' the order.

8.10.2. Review of compensation orders

The court may discharge or reduce compensation orders on limited statutory grounds. The most frequently used ground is that 'the defendant has suffered a substantial reduction of his means which was unexpected at the time when the order was made and that his means seem unlikely to increase for a considerable period'. The difference with altering fines is that a compensation review cannot normally go ahead immediately and the outstanding balance can extend to 2 years, or exceptionally 3 years of instalments. The compensatee must be notified and allowed to make representations at the review hearing as to the proposed discharge or reduction, and the reason should be given, e.g. the change in financial circumstances. Representations may be made in writing. In reality, the compensatees are very often local councils in respect of damage, and insurance companies who have paid out the victim. Responses are rare. Compensatees should be made aware that they may still claim any balance or full amount in the County Court even if the order is discharged.

8.11. One day detention

A flexible friend. Distinguish this option from 'imprisonment'! It is available for default as described above, and also as a penalty for imprisonable offences. It enables the court to detain within the precincts of the court or at any police station until 8 p.m. as a primary sentence, or in default of paying a fine (including the 18 to 21 age group). The custody criteria do not apply. Nevertheless it is a restriction on liberty and if a lengthy period is considered, it may be appropriate to allow consultation with the duty solicitor.

Examples:

- Detention in the court room 'until the court rises' for an offence at a 'fine entry point' where there is an inability to pay but some punishment is appropriate. N.B. must be imprisonable.
- Detention 'deemed already served' in respect of defendants/defaulters who have already spent a night in the cells and this satisfies the seriousness of the offence.
- Detention until 8 p.m. in police cells in respect of an offence e.g. failure to surrender to bail for a defendant who has no previous convictions and has surrendered voluntarily to a warrant after getting the dates confused. The penalty may carry a more forceful message than a fine, and it distinguishes the outcome of an arrest on warrant, i.e. he is detained in the cells on warrant prior to the hearing, and then remains afterwards as the sentence for the offence.
- Detention with release after the conclusion of the case as a method of wiping out outstanding costs/excise penalties which cannot be remitted.

8.12. Disqualification from driving

Another flexible friend, which is now available as a penalty in its own right for any offence - endorseable or not. For example, it may be used as a sole penalty for the traffic offender who already has substantial fines which are going to take another 12 months to pay. It may also be an appropriate method of dealing meaningfully with fly-tippers and kerb crawler, or indeed anyone who is driving a motor vehicle as part and parcel of his means of offending. See also at 8.46.

OFFENCE IS 'SERIOUS ENOUGH'

The following offences are examples of offences which are considered to be 'serious enough' to carry an entry point of community penalty in the Sentencing Guidelines:

Burglary of non-dwelling; common assault; possess class A drugs; cultivation of cannabis; failure to surrender to bail; going equipped for theft; obtaining by deception; false representation to obtain benefit; taking motor vehicle without owner's consent; theft; vehicle interference; drive whilst disqualified; driving with alcohol/breath reading between 86-115 ml (well over twice the limit to just over three times the limit.

8.13.   Sentencing options for offences committed <u>on or before</u> 4th April 2005

These sentences will continue to be imposed for some time to come, particularly where warrants are outstanding for old offences.

Type of Order	Main features of the Order
Attendance Centre Order	Offence must be imprisonable 18 to 20 year old males only 12 hours to 36 hours (Usually 3 hours per week or fortnight)
Community Punishment Order (CPO) *Formerly a Community Service Order*	Offence must be imprisonable 40 hours to 240 hours order Between 5 hours and 21 hours per week
Community Rehabilitation Order (CRO) *Formerly a Probation Order*	6 months to 3 years. Weekly supervision appointments for 12 weeks, then fortnightly for 12 weeks, then monthly May include requirements, e.g. to comply with accredited programmes curfew, residence
Community Punishment and Rehabilitation Order (CPRO) *Also known as a Combination Order*	CRO element must be at least 12 months CPO element no more than 100 hours
Intensive Change and Control Programme (ICCP) Specified areas only.	18 - 20 year old males and females only CPRO + curfew, including 18+ hours per week of structured activity and mentoring for 1st 3 months, then reducing

Curfew Order with electronic monitoring	Remain indoors at specified place(s) and times. Monitoring by electronic tag 2 - 12 hours per day for up to 6 months
Drug Treatment and Testing Order	Dependant on or propensity to misuse drugs. Requires and may be susceptible to treatment. Offender's consent required. Treatment and Testing - at least 2 samples per week for 1st 13 weeks - results provided to monthly reviews by the court. Supervision - 12 hours (low intensity order) to 20+ hours (high) of activities for 1st 13 weeks, then reducing. High restriction on liberty must be proportionate. 6 months to 3 years.

Although all the above Orders now have a close equivalent as a requirement within a community order, there is at least one difference in the main features of each option, except the curfew requirement which is identical.

8.13.1. Breach of orders made for offences before 4th April 2005

The options are as follows:

- No action taken by the court. This is rare, but may well be encouraged by the responsible probation officer who is obliged to bring the case to court because of two breaches under National Standards guidance. The officer may feel confident that the defendant will comply in future and a disciplinary fine may exacerbate the very problem which the order is trying to address. A clear warning by the court may be sufficient to encourage completion of the order.
- Fine not exceeding £1000 (Guideline entry point is band B).
- Community punishment order for up to 60 hours (maximum aggregate = 240 hours). The addition of extra hours for a breach of community punishment is a valuable option.
- Attendance centre order for breach of community rehabilitation order only.
- Revoke and re-sentence - custody may be imposed if there has been wilful and persistent refusal to comply with a Magistrates' Court order (provided that the original offence carries imprisonment), but committal to Crown Court would be necessary for a Crown Court order to be revoked and re-sentenced.

Application may also be made for amendment and revocation. Note that breach options on the new community order are very different (see 8.28)! As with the making of 'old orders', the period for dealing with the lifetimes of the old orders makes it well worthwhile to have the 'old breach provisions' to hand.

8.14. Sentencing options for offences committed <u>after</u> 5th April 2005 - 'serious enough' offence.

8.14.1. Fine/Discharge

Fines and discharges are available as before, but the fine may be imposed within any of the sentencing bands.

'Sentencers must consider all of the disposals available at the time of sentence, so that even where the threshold for community sentence has been passed a financial penalty or discharge may still be an appropriate penalty.... Recent improvements in enforcement of financial penalties make them a more viable sentence in a wider range of cases' (Sentencing Guidelines Council).

8.14.2. Community order (CO)

This order replaces all previous community sentences as described at 8.13 as a single generic order.

8.14.3. Period of community order

The period of the community order must be specified. There is no prescribed minimum but there is a maximum of 3 years. If a supervision requirement is included, then it must last for the same length as the order, i.e. the supervision must extend to the end of the order. It is not therefore possible to make a community order with a curfew requirement for 6 months and supervision for only 3 months - the supervision must extend to the full extent of 6 months.

Normally the community order period will be determined by the longest requirement, e.g. supervision for 6 months would be a 6 month order, unpaid work hours would be within a 12 month period. Similarly, a single requirement of a 4 month curfew would mean a 4 month community order.

In theory the community order could extend for a longer period than its longest requirement, e.g. for 6 months, so that any breaches could be dealt with by simply adding into the period left over. However, this means that the offender has the responsibility to 'keep in touch' with the responsible officer and notify changes of address basically in a vacuum, and would be liable to be re-sentenced during that period even if has completed the requirements faultlessly. Apart from which is it is a rather pessimistic reason to make an order longer - just in case there is a breach and the court may need a longer period to add other requirements. It would be an interesting calculation to consider just how much longer a particular defendant should be given. A debatable point! See 8.28.

In fixing the duration of the order, the court may have regard to any period spent in custody for that offence, and the SGC recommends that the period should be taken into account in all cases, or explain why it is not justified. For instance, the defendant has been on remand in custody for several weeks and the punishment elements of a curfew and unpaid work requirement should be reduced on this basis.

8.14.4. Types of requirements

The restriction on liberty must be commensurate with the seriousness of the offence. The requirements must be considered to be the most suitable for the offender and they must be compatible with each other e.g. a curfew period must not prevent a specified activity. It is therefore necessary to seek this information through the probation service by report.

The available requirements are as follows, with their closest previous equivalents:

Requirements in a CO	Closest previous equivalent
Unpaid work	Community Punishment Order
Supervision	Community Rehabilitation Order (CRO)
Curfew	Curfew Order
Attendance Centre	Attendance Centre Order
Residence	Requirement of a CRO
Accredited programmes	Same programmes - requirement of a CRO
Alcohol treatment	Requirement of a CRO
Mental health treatment	Requirement of a CRO
Drug Rehabilitation Requirement (DRR)	Part only of a Drug Treatment and Testing Order
Specified activity	New
Prohibited activity	New
Exclusion	New

8.14.5. High, medium and low range

The community order is further sophisticated by the calculation of whether the order should be pitched at a low, medium or high level of restriction. In very broad terms, the starting point is that there should normally be only one requirement at the low level; one or two requirements at medium; and up to three requirements at high level - or equivalent restriction by increasing/reducing duration of the requirement. For example, unpaid work at high level would normally be 150 hours if combined with other requirements, but could be up to 300 hours if it was the only requirement at that level (see 8.27). In determining this, the seriousness of the offence is obviously 'an important factor' and will give a preliminary indicator.

The court must also be guided by the:

- Purpose of the sentence
- Risk of re-offending
- Ability of the offender to comply and
- Availability of requirements locally (SGC).

These are all aspects which the probation service are in a position to explore. The court therefore can only be expected to give a provisional assessment when seeking a report from probation. It will almost always be necessary to ensure that the court has full flexibility to make any sentence at all when it is later in possession of the full facts, i.e. to state that the sentencing court will not be bound to sentence within the provisional banding. The purpose may change from punishment to rehabilitation if the probation service discover a drug or drink problem. The risk of re-offending may increase with a disclosure made in interview, and further restriction may be sought. It may also be possible that the defendant is not suitable for any of the community order requirements envisaged!

The court therefore makes a provisional assessment based on offence information with limited offender information so that probation have a clear starting point. This may be based on perceptions of purpose, the seriousness level, any specific issues which have emerged or even specific requirements if the bench is sufficiently inspired at this stage. For instance, a request to probation to consider drug/alcohol/domestic violence/mental health issues at high level; or explore rehabilitation and protection requirements at medium level, or to consider a low level unpaid work requirement. It is important to ensure that the defendant is aware that the final sentence remains open for when the full offender picture is obtained from probation. The various requirements are discussed below and a table of the suggested requirements and duration at each level is at 8.27 (SGC).

8.14.6. Duties of the offender in all community orders

The offender must keep in touch with the responsible officer in accordance with instructions and must notify any change of address. Both of these duties are enforceable as requirements in all community orders and should be announced clearly. Many offenders do not have settled accommodation and the notification of change of address is one of the most important points to make in order to avoid missed correspondence and the time-consuming tracking if the order is breached.

8.14.7. Responsible officer allocated

One or more 'responsible officers' are allocated to each community order, and their duty is to promote compliance and enforce if necessary. Normally this will be a probation officer, but it may be someone else e.g. attendance centre officer, electronic monitoring contractor.

8.14.8. Probation report - Fast Delivery and Standard Delivery

A probation report will normally be required before the court can make a community order, so that suitability for particular requirements, and risk of harm can be assessed. There are two types of report. Firstly, the Fast Delivery Report which was previously known as a 'stand-down' report or 'specific sentence report'. This report can normally be prepared on the day of sentence if the case is stood down from the list for about an hour. Alternatively it can be prepared within a few days, depending upon local resources. The report is adequate for low level, most medium level orders, and also straightforward requirements such as unpaid work, curfew and supervision.

Secondly, there is the more detailed Standard Delivery Report, previously known as the full pre-sentence report. This will normally take 3/4 weeks to prepare and will assess the wider picture in order to determine the most suitable and effective outcome within the seriousness band. Cases involving domestic violence, sexual offences, mental health, serious drug use and alcoholism will normally require this level of enquiry and background information. A Standard Delivery Report will always be required if custody remains an option, unless a report is considered to be unnecessary (see 8.31).

Types of requirements:

8.15.   Unpaid work

The offender must perform work at the times as instructed by the responsible officer.

Criteria:

- The court must be satisfied that the offender is suitable to perform work - usually following a probation report
- The requirement must be performed within 12 months.

There are various issues to consider in respect of suitability. It may be appropriate for an offender to undertake only light duties if there is some illness or disability which may be a bar to full time work but not to one day per week. Work sessions must not prevent or conflict with employment, benefit entitlement, religion or cultural requirements. The work will be allocated on the basis of an individual assessment. For instance, a low risk offender with a specific skill may be allocated to a single task with low level supervision. A sex offender may be allocated to a single gender team away from busy public areas. An offender with communication problems and aggressive tendencies may be unable to work with six other adults in a team and he may need individual supervision.

The aim of the selected tasks for unpaid work is to create a visible benefit to the community and also to the offender e.g. the change from wasteland to a garden producing vegetables for charitable use. There is a wide range of potential work e.g. painting, decorating, gardening, cooking and serving at luncheon clubs, assisting with riding for the disabled, removal of graffiti, stocking and sales in charity shops.

The potential benefits include introduction or re-introduction to the work ethic; responding to the positive role-modelling by the supervisor who has high contact time; practical problem solving as a team, and learning new skills. The hours may include 20% for basic literacy or directly related qualifications e.g. health and safety.

- 40 hours - 300 hours (60 hours longer limit than the CPO)
- Minimum average of 6 hours per week - incudes travel time in excess of half hour each way, and half hour for lunch on site (National Standards).

8.16. Supervision

The offender must attend appointments with the responsible officer, or another person determined by the relevant officer, for the purpose of rehabilitation.

It is important to realise that none of the other requirements automatically carry a supervision requirement. It must be specifically added. This is particularly relevant to the accredited programmes which previously could only come along with a community rehabilitation order. Virtually every programme will need a supervision requirement to build up to, support and deal with the aftermath of attendance on any of the programmes. Similarly it will be necessary for offenders who need support beyond the 'straight' drug rehabilitation requirement.

The potential benefits are that supervision is based on individual needs, rather than group needs, and other agencies and facilities are frequently accessed through this relationship. It is a regular one to one support mechanism, particularly during the early weeks after sentence when the potential for change is at it's highest.

- No minimum period - maximum of 3 years
- Must always extend to the full period of the community order
- Minimum of one contact per week to 16 weeks, and then as defined by offender manager (National Standards).

8.17. Electronic curfew

The offender must remain for periods specified at a place. This may include different periods for different days and specify different addresses, e.g. weekly address with night curfew and weekend address with daytime curfew.

Criteria:

- The court must obtain and consider information about the place proposed (including the attitude of persons likely to be affected by the enforced presence of the offender). This is likely to be dealt with so far as practicable as a fast delivery report. Realistically, if there are problems with other occupiers, it may be necessary to apply for early revocation of the requirement.
- The court must also impose an electronic monitoring requirement unless arrangements are not yet agreed locally, or it is inappropriate to do so. If it is the only requirement, the 'responsible officer' will be the contractor.

Subject to local arrangements, the contractor will normally fit the tag and install the telephone equipment within the first couple of curfew periods. The curfew itself is in place from the outset - tag or not. The range of electronic monitoring will normally allow the offender to stand outside to 'take the air' and smoke. If he is not in range during the curfew period, this will be relayed on screen at the contractor's headquarters and action will be taken. The contractor will deal with telephone and written warnings, and breaches for interference with the tag, damage to the equipment and failures to comply with the curfew.

The potential benefits are that it may be used as pure punishment with a nightly curfew, or as a preventative restriction on liberty during the individual's peak offending times. It has great flexibility and lifestyles may change in the longer term.

Example: Weekend binge drinking is the basis of the offending behaviour.

Curfew with monitoring on Fridays from 5 p.m. to 5 a.m. and Saturdays between 2 p.m. and 2 a.m. A targeted two-day curfew may be more useful at critical times - especially 'happy hours' and Saturday afternoons if appropriate. A curfew for 2 days per week for 6 months compares to a daily curfew for 6 weeks, of say 7 p.m. to 7 a.m. which may only change normal behaviour at the weekend in any event. It can properly deal with seriousness level and enables credit to be given for a guilty plea. The report writer needs to be alerted to the purpose of the curfew so that relevant information is available to the court e.g. drinking patterns.

- 🕐 2 hours to 12 hours per day
- 🕐 No minimum. Maximum of 6 months.

8.18. Accredited programmes

The offender must participate in a specified accredited programme at a place specified and on the number of days specified.

Criteria:
- The court is satisfied that the programme is available as specified
- Probation must recommend the programme as being suitable
- Any third parties involved must consent
- The offender must comply with the instructions of the person in charge of the programme.

Examples:

- *General Offending Programme (GOP) - 'Think First' / 'Enhanced Thinking Skills' (ETS) / Priestley 'One to One' (POTO).*

20 intensive group work sessions (except Priestley version). The overall aim is to prevent re-offending by improving the thinking skills of the offender. It is based on the premise that thinking is the basis of all behaviour, so in order to affect or change criminal behaviour, the underlying thoughts and attitudes of offenders must be addressed. The skills of thinking in certain areas such as self-control, problem-solving, creative thinking, critical reasoning and seeing things from another person's point of view.

The Enhanced Thinking Skills programme was originally developed by the Prison Service and evidenced a 15% reduction in re-convictions. Psychometric tests are undertaken, before and after the programme to measure change.

- *Drink Impaired Drivers (DIDs)*

16 group work sessions. The objectives include increasing factual knowledge about the effects of alcohol; encouraging a constructive change in attitude; developing awareness of strategies to resist undue pressure to drink more than they wish; enabling them to recognise implications of drinking on themselves and others and the effect on essential driving skills. Many drivers chose to attend a voluntary course offered by the court so that their disqualification period is reduced. The reality is that when the time comes to attend the course, many are either unwilling to pay the fee, or find that they have managed without a licence and await the natural end of the disqualification instead of attending. The accredited programme is court ordered and can result in breach proceedings. There is also no harm in attending both!

Other programmes are:

- Addressing Substance Related Offending (ASRO) - 20 sessions. The aim is to help reduce and stop illegal drug and problematic alcohol use and reduce associated crime. The focus is on dealing with the triggers to drug and alcohol use rather than the use of the substances themselves. It is rarely recommended as 'first base' for drug users, as treatment and support is usually required before the discipline of attending a programme can realistically be expected.
- Integrated Domestic Abuse Programme (IDAP) - 24 sessions. The aim is to focus on control and misuse of power, and it addresses both physical and psychological violence. The victim's needs are supported throughout the programme with a co-ordinated effort by all relevant agencies including the police.
- Sex Offenders Programme - This teaches new attitudes and behaviours, and enables the offender to recognise the danger signals and to act on them.

8.19. Drug Rehabilitation Requirement (DRR)

The statutory purpose of the DRR is 'reduction or elimination of offender's dependency or propensity to use drugs'. Note that the requirement is not necessarily expected to achieve total success. In practical terms, the reduction, if not total elimination of offending, is a realistic aim. Samples are provided by the offender of the description and at such times/circumstances as directed in order to determine if he has any drug in his body.

Criteria:

- Offender is dependent on, or has propensity to misuse drugs and may be susceptible to treatment
- Arrangements are made/can be made for treatment as a resident or non-resident, by or under the direction of a specified person

- Offender must consent
- Probation officer recommends DRR as being suitable
- Periodic reviews by the court may be ordered with a report by the responsible officer with test results, at least monthly - only obligatory if the DRR is more than 12 months duration.

The DRR is <u>not</u> an equivalent of the Drug Treatment and Testing Order (pre-April 2005). At the low level it is little more than weekly testing with the treatment element potentially limited to provision of a prescription, with the involvement of a key worker or general practitioner. A DRR does not carry automatic supervision, accredited programme or court reviews.

The DRR is therefore available to a far wider group of offenders with lower offending profiles than the DTTO. As a general guide defendants will be selected by the probation service for assessment if they are currently using a class A drug at least weekly, but others may also be suitable.

There may well be existing drug treatment and support delivered by Criminal Justice Integrated Teams (CJITs) through the Drug Interventions Programme (DIP), whether as a condition of bail in pilot areas, or on a voluntary basis, especially following criminal charge. This is an important route into a DRR, rather than a competing intervention and the probation report will give details of action taken and progress prior to sentence. Any treatment and case management will be taken over by the DRR treatment provider if a community order is made. The treatment must not be specified in the order.

The lack of offender motivation should no longer be a reason for failing to propose a DRR unless it is clear that there will be no compliance and/or there is no consent. It is now recognised that building motivation is part of the support task.

Offenders will normally be tested at least twice per week for the first 16 weeks, with reduction to weekly testing if sufficient progress is made (National Standards). Testing might not always be on the same day(s) of each week and the testing method may vary from oral fluid to urine. Urine tests no longer have to be observed, as was the case with DTTOs. Offenders may sign to admit drug use rather than undergo the drug test. Positive drug tests in themselves are not a ground for breach and there is an expectation that there will be a period with some positive tests at the outset. However, positive tests can be indicative of a failure to engage in the programme and repeated failures will be brought back to court for revocation and re-sentence.

If court reviews are ordered, a report will be produced by the offender manager every 4 weeks for the first 16 weeks and then at least every 16 weeks afterwards, and this will include the test results (National Standards). The court will follow progress, encourage, motivate, and if necessary, warn. The review hearing may also deal with breach, amendment and revocation/re-sentence.

- Treatment and testing for at least 6 months - maximum 3 years
- At least 2 samples per week must be provided during first 16 weeks, with reduction to 1 sample per week if sufficient progress made (1 sample per week at a low level DRR)

- ⏰ Total contact time for <u>all</u> requirements in an order which includes DRR, i.e. most drug users will realistically need supervision and, at high level, an accredited programme as well:
  Low = one contact per week, but no minimum hours
  Medium = at least 8 hours per week for the first 16 weeks
  High = at least 15 hours per week for the first 16 weeks.

8.20. Attendance Centre

Offenders under the age of 25 must attend at a specified attendance centre for a specified number of hours.

- The court must be satisfied that the centre is reasonably accessible to the offender, having regard to the means of access available to him and any other circumstances. Some court areas are basically unable to use this option if there is not a sufficiently local centre.

The Officer in Charge of the centre fixes the dates and times of attendance, having regard to the offender's circumstances.

The regime 'shall include a programme of group activities designed to assist offenders to acquire or develop personal responsibility, self-discipline, skills and interests'. This is also a useful option to add to an existing order if there is a breach of other requirements.

- ⏰ 12 hours to 36 hours for up to 3 hours per session.

8.21. Residence

A requirement that during a period specified, the offender must reside at a place specified in the order. If the order so provides, the requirement does not prohibit the offender from moving address with the prior approval of the responsible officer.

- The home surroundings of the offender must be considered.
- The court may not specify a hostel or other institution except on the recommendation of the probation officer.

Residence in approved premises (formerly described as probation/bail hostels) carries an obligation to abide by the rules and curfew. The residence may equally be at a private address.

- ⏰ Up to 3 years.

8.22. Alcohol treatment

The offender must submit during the specified period to treatment directed by a specified qualified/experienced person with a view to reduction or elimination of offender's dependency on alcohol.

Criteria:

- The offender is dependent on alcohol
- The dependency is such as requires and may be susceptible to treattment
- Arrangements have been/can be made for the treatment
- Offender must consent
- Treatment may be resident at specified place, or non-resident at specified intervals.

The actual treatment must not be specified. The treatment requirement is predominantly medical-based rather than behaviour-based which would be dealt with by attendance on a specialised programme e.g. ASRO (8.18), or a relevant specified activity. The models of care will depend upon the individual and the assessment of medium or high level restriction. The type of intervention ranges from advice by a specialist nurse, use of Alcoholics Anonymous, through to prescriptions for assisted withdrawal, psychological therapies, and at the highest tier of offender, to in-patient assisted withdrawal. Any testing is on an entirely voluntary basis.

⏲ Minimum period of 6 months to 3 years.

8.23. Mental health treatment

The offender must submit during the specified period to treatment directed by a specified registered medical practitioner and/or a chartered psychologist, with a view to the improvement of the offender's mental condition.

Criteria:

- The court is satisfied on the evidence of an approved registered medical practitioner that the mental condition requires and may be susceptible to treatment, but is not such as to warrant the making of a hospital or guardianship order (see below)
- Arrangements have been/can be made for the treatment
- Offender must consent

The treatment may be as a resident or non-resident patient in a hospital or care home, but not where high security psychiatric services are provided. The offender may be transferred to another place for treatment by consent if appropriate. The actual treatment must not be specified.

⏲ No minimum. Up to 3 years maximum.

The court may also consider two alternative sentences when dealing with defendants suffering from mental disorder. Both options require the evidence of two registered medical practitioners to make the recommendation. Firstly, the Hospital Order which involves detention in hospital. It will normally lapse after six months, but the mental health authorities may extend the period or discharge early. The period is not a matter for the court. Secondly, the

Guardianship Order. The defendant is effectively handed over from the court as a patient to the mental health authorities under the guardianship of a social worker or person approved by the local authority. In some cases it may be appropriate to ensure that these options are left open for the medical professionals to explore if a case is adjourned primarily to consider a community order requirement.

8.24. Specified activity

The offender must present himself to a specified person at a specified place on specified days and participate in specified activity in accordance with the instructions of the person in charge.

The activities may include activities whose purpose is reparation and involve contact between offenders and victims.

Criteria:

- The court must consult a probation officer
- Be satisfied that it is feasible to secure compliance with the requirement
- Any third parties must consent to be involved

Examples - Specified activities (subject to local provision)

Group work to deal with anger management, fire raisers, racial and religious awareness; attendance at a day centre; employment training and basic literacy/numeracy at a local college; debt counselling at a citizen's advice bureau; mediation with the victim of the crime; one to one mentoring.

Attendance is measured in 'days' and each attendance counts as 'a day' even though it may not necessarily be for a full day. If the requirement cannot be measured exactly, it may well be worded 'for up to xx days' to allow some flexibility and assessment of progress.

⏲ No minimum. Aggregate days must not exceed 60 days.

825. Prohibited activity

The offender must refrain from participating in activities specified in the order on a day or days specified or during a specified period.

- The court must consult a probation officer
- The requirements may include a requirement that the offender does not possess, use or carry a prohibited firearm.

Examples - Prohibited activities

Not to attend specified football matches (less restrictive than a football banning order); Not to drink alcohol on the public highway; Not to carry paint aerosols or felt tip pens; Not to communicate with the victim in any way.

See below at 8.26 regarding the practicalities of enforcement.

⏲ No minimum. Up to 3 years.

8.26. Exclusion requirement

The offender is prohibited from entering a place or area specified in the order for a period so specified.

- The requirement may provide for the prohibition to operate only during the periods specified in the order and may specify different places for different periods or days.

Examples - Exclusion requirements

Not to enter NCP car parks; Not to go within 100 metres of the victim's home/ place of work; Not to enter the xx shopping centre.

If there are serious issues about prevention and protection, it may well be more appropriate to consider a specific ancillary order e.g. Anti Social Behaviour Order, Sex Offences Protection Order, Football Banning Order. The requirements on these ancillary orders are sent immediately to the police for recording on the Police National Computer and the police are then aware, or can easily check any violation of prohibited actions or exclusions.

Since August 2005, a constable has been able to direct a person to leave an exclusion area and if the direction is contravened, the constable may arrest the offender. The offence of knowingly contravening a direction to leave an exclusion area as defined in a community order or suspended sentence, carries custody. The difficulty is that there is, as yet, no national procedure for notification of the exclusion requirement details to the police. Victims may obviously be made aware specifically so that they may contact the police on breach, but the police would normally be relying on checking then with court records. Electronic monitoring is currently being piloted for exclusions.

⏲ No minimum. Up to 2 years.

8.27. Community order menu - proportionality between 'high/medium/ low' orders

The periods quoted in the table below are based upon Sentencing Guidelines Council suggestions and the National Implementation Guide for the National Offender Management Service. Note that the Attendance Centre requirement only appears at low seriousness as a single requirement, and the accredited programmes, residence, mental health, and alcohol treatment do not appear in the low level group. Mental health and alcohol treatment have the potential for high restriction and the actual requirement for the individual should be checked for proportionality with the offending level.

Seriousness	
HIGH	**Normally 1 - 3 requirements** **Consider overall restriction on liberty.** • Unpaid work – 150 to 300 hours • Supervision – 12 months to 3 years • Electronic curfew – up to 12 hours per day for 4 to 6 months • Accredited programme - *Addressing Substance Related Offending (ASRO); Enhanced Thinking Skills (ETS); Think First; Priestley One to One; Integrated Domestic Abuse Programme; Drink Impaired Drivers (DIDs); Sex Offenders Programme.* • Drug Rehabilitation Requirement (DRR) *At high level - with Supervision (12 months - 3 years) + ASRO programme.* *2 samples per week. 15 hours + total contact per week. Monthly review obligatory.* • Specified activity – up to 60 days • Exclusion without monitoring - normally 'about' 12 months (max 2 years) • Prohibited activity – normally up to 12 months (max 3 years) • Residence • Alcohol Treatment • Mental Health Treatment
MEDIUM	**Normally 1 or 2 requirements.** • Unpaid work – 80 to 150 hours • Supervision – 12 to 18 months • Electronic curfew – up to 12 hours per day for 2 to 3 months • Accredited programme - *Addressing Substance Related Offending (ASRO); Enhanced Thinking Skills (ETS); Think First; Priestley One to One; Integrated Domestic Abuse Programme; Drink Impaired Drivers (DIDs); Sex Offenders Programme.* • Drug Rehabilitation Requirement (DRR) - *At medium level - with Supervision (6 to 12 months).* *2 samples per week. 8 hours + total contact per week.* *Monthly court reviews optional to 12 months/ obligatory at 12 months.* • Specified activity – 20 to 30 days • Exclusion without monitoring – up to 6 months • Prohibited activity – up to 6 months • Residence • Alcohol Treatment • Mental Health Treatment

Seriousness	Normally 1 requirement only or curtail the length.
LOW	• Unpaid work – 40 to 80 hours • Supervision – up to 12 months (no minimum period specified) • Electronic curfew – up to 12 hours per day for 4 to 6 weeks • Drug Rehabilitation Requirement (DRR) – must consent *At low level - as a single requirement - 1 or 2 samples per week for up to 6 months; under direction of doctor or key worker.* • Specified activity - up to 12 days • Exclusion without monitoring – up to 3 months • Prohibited activity – up to 3 months • Attendance Centre - 12 to 36 hours.

8.28. Breach of community order

- **Warning and court action**

If the responsible officer is of the opinion that the offender has failed without reasonable excuse to comply with any requirements, the officer must give a warning. The exceptions are if there has previously been a warning in the last 12 months, when court action must be taken, or court action is considered to be more appropriate even for a first breach. The starting point is that any failures are deemed by the officer to be unacceptable unless the offender provides an explanation within 7 days.

If court action is to be taken, i.e. 2nd failure within 12 months or a serious 1st breach, then proceedings will be instigated within 10 days, with the issue of a summons or warrant.

Most breach proceedings concern either failing to attend appointments or failing to notify a change of address which is an important requirement of all community orders. The remainder involve failing to comply with particular instructions, e.g. failing to work as instructed, failing to provide a medical certificate within 7 days of a failure to attend a supervision appointment. The Magistrates' Court may also deal with breaches of Crown Court orders if the order gives that permission. Other orders are preserved to the Crown Court for action.

- **Primary objective in sentencing for breach of community order**

The primary objective is to ensure that the order is actually completed and the purpose of the sentence is therefore achieved. The court is encouraged to consider alternatives within the range of the community order and leave custody as a last resort. The custodial period for a community order, particularly if made within the 'serious enough' band cannot justifiably be for a long period. Seriousness was fixed below the custody band. The purpose also contracts to one of pure punishment - usually far shorter than the community order, and potentially far less onerous. The new powers reflect this new philosophy.

- **Powers of the court**

  ☐ Amend the terms of the order so as to impose more onerous requirements which the court could include if it were then making the order. Any new requirements must be within the minimum and maximum periods, e.g. unpaid work cannot be added unless it is at least 40 hours. If the unpaid work is in existence already, then the order can be varied from 40 hours to 50 hours as the minimum is satisfied. The requirements may be extended, but not beyond the period of the community order as fixed at the outset. There is specific provision to extend the period of 12 months for the completion of unpaid work.

Examples:

1. *Breach of a community order with 80 hours unpaid work requirement. Possibilities - amend from 80 hours to 90 hours unpaid work; amend by adding a 10 day specified activity; amend by adding a 28 day curfew requirement.*

2. *Breach of a community order with 12 months supervision requirement. Possibilities - amend by including the minimum of 40 hours unpaid work, but this would be very onerous as a breach outcome; add curfew*

  ☐ Where the order was made by the Magistrates' Court, by revoking the order and dealing with him for the offence in any way in which the court could have dealt with him at the time of conviction. This may include the making of a new community order.

Examples

1. *Breach of a single requirement of a 12 week curfew at the 10th week does not allow for a meaningful extension, or addition of another penalty, as the community order will expire in 2 weeks time. A revocation and re-sentence for an 8 week curfew may be an appropriate outcome. This effectively means that the curfew will run for an additional 6 weeks.*

2. *Compare if the curfew was a 2nd requirement alongside a 12 month supervision requirement. The community order is therefore in existence for another 9 months and there is ample time for an amendment of the existing curfew. It could be varied from 12 weeks to 18 weeks - an additional 6 weeks.*

  ☐ If the original offence was not imprisonable, the re-sentence may be custody if the offender has wilfully and persistently failed to comply with the requirements, e.g. revocation of the order and imprisonment of 28 days instead for a 3rd breach.

  ☐ Where the order was made by the Crown Court, it may be dealt with for breach in the Magistrates' Court if there is a relevant direction for breach action in the Magistrates' Court. However, when re-sentence is envisaged, the case may be committed on bail or in custody to the Crown Court, along with a certificate as to the failure.

The court must take into consideration the extent to which the offender has complied with the order in determining the breach penalty. The SGC states that orders should not be so overloaded that breach is precipitated.

It is legally possible to make the community order for a longer period than the longest provision so that there is some space for additional requirements if breached. There are difficulties with this, including, how long is long enough? Another 12 months to cater for the possibility of unpaid work being added in later)? Would a court really re-sentence on a further conviction if the requirements were complete? See further at 8.14.3.

Note that there is no longer any power to 'take no action' or to fine. These outcomes are confined to enforcement of the old orders.

8.29. Revocation and amendment of community orders

The offender or responsible officer may apply to revoke or amend the order. Revocation may result in either total revocation e.g. based upon good progress, or revocation and re-sentence e.g. illness prevents compliance with an unpaid work requirement and a supervision requirement is imposed instead. Amendment of an order may involve cancellation of requirements or replacement of requirements, e.g. a change of treatment, extension of 12 months for unpaid work to be completed, drug reviews to be heard in absence in future.

8.30. Subsequent conviction during community order

If the offender is convicted of another offence during the period of the order and it appears to be in the interests of justice, having regard to the circumstances which have arisen, the court may revoke the order or revoke and re-sentence.

Examples:

1. The new offence merits lengthy custody, so there cannot be compliance with the community order in any event. Revocation and re-sentence to a short concurrent or consecutive custodial sentence may be considered. The period would depend upon the extent of compliance. Virtual completion might possibly be dealt with simply by revocation without re-sentencing at all.

2. The new offence merits a community order. Consideration may be given to revoking the old order and re-sentencing with a new community order which includes the balance of the previous requirements so that there is a single concurrent order for the old and new matters.

OFFENCE IS 'SO SERIOUS'

The following offences are examples of 'custody' entry points in the sentencing guidelines:

Affray; aggravated vehicle-taking; assault occasioning actual bodily harm; assault on police officer; breach of anti-social behaviour order; harassment causing fear of violence; indecent assault; possess offensive weapon; theft in breach of trust; dangerous driving; driving with breath/alcohol limit over 116ml (well over 3 times the limit).

Note that more serious offences are designated as an entry point of committal to Crown Court e.g. domestic burglary, supply of class A drugs.

The penalties open to the court at the 'so serious' level are: Fine, Community Order, custody, suspended sentence or intermittent custody

- Fine - This is likely to be rare, but it is legal.

- Community order - This may well be appropriate for a high level community order, particularly if the purpose is drug rehabilitation. Custody cannot address drug rehabilitation within the reality of living in the community. The alternative option of a suspended sentence is likely to be breached and activated during the early stages of treatment. A high community order at this level should be clearly marked as such so that if re-sentence on breach becomes inevitable, the court can properly consider the full extent of a custodial sentence as a starting point. . The SGC also give the example of a defendant where custody is warranted but he has served on remand and a community order with supervision may be appropriate as a penalty.

8.31. Custody

Defendants aged 21 and over will serve the custodial sentence as imprisonment in a prison. Defendants aged 18 to 21 will serve their custodial sentence as 'detention' in a Young Offenders Institution.
The restriction on imposing custody is now as follows:

- The offence, or a combination of the offence and one or more associated offences are 'so serious' that neither a fine alone nor a community sentence can be justified for the offence.

- Failure to express willingness to comply with a requirement which is proposed by the court to be included in a community order and which requires an expression of such willingness.

A Standard Delivery Report is required unless it is considered to be 'unnecessary'. It may be considered to be unnecessary if, for instance, a recent report is available, or a very short period is to be imposed and the defendant has previously served custodial sentences.

The court must announce reasons and record them on the register and commitment. This will usually consist of the list of aggravating features. There are three practical effects to explain. Firstly, there will be a half remission subject to good behaviour. Secondly, in respect of offences committed from 4th April 2005, the prison service now supply details of the period spent on remand in custody and the court must consider the number of days to be taken into account. Normally the full period will be allowed (SGC). Reasons must be given if the period is reduced, if the court considers that it is not just to take them into account, e.g. excessive prevarication so that custodial sentence would be served effectively as a remand prisoner. Days will not be counted if the remand days are in respect of an earlier offence or spent on prison recall after breaching the licence.

Thirdly, the court must explain the power to order a return to custody if a further offence is committed during the balance of the sentence. Importantly, at the present time, licence provisions do not apply to full-time sentences which are less than 12 months, i.e. no licence provisions with any custodial sentence imposed in the Magistrates' Court (except intermittent custody - below).

- Minimum = 5 days imprisonment (7 days for fine defaulters)/21 days detention for offenders aged 18 to 21.
- Maximum = 6 months (or statutory maximum if less) for single offence/ 12 months for 2+ either-way offences.
- Remission at half way through the sentence, subject to good behaviour.
- Release prior to remission period, on Home Detention Curfew (HDC). As a starting point, this applies to virtually all offences sentenced in the Magistrates' Court, subject to grant by prison governor. The defendant must serve 30 days minimum in custody, and thereafter, one quarter of the sentence, e.g. release on tag at 30 days applies to both a 3 and 4 months sentence. The HDC applies up to the half way point when the remission period begins.

8.31.1. Intermittent custody (pilot areas only)

The custody criteria must be met. Intermittent custody enables the defendant to be punished with a restriction of liberty of up to 4 days per week, alongside keeping and developing their life in the community, as a family member, employee etc. for the remainder of the week. The adapted prisons are HMP Morton Hall, Lincoln for women and HMP Kirkham, Preston for men. Throughout the overall sentence the defendant is subject to licence conditions, which will normally be suggested in the pre-sentence report, e.g. supervision, electronic curfew. The custodial criteria must be satisfied. There is no remission as such, and Home Detention Curfew therefore applies to the very end, rather than just to the half way point. Approved travelling expenses are paid to and from prison. A breach for failure to comply with requirements or failure to arrive at the prison may result in application to court to vary to full-time custody.

- Overall sentence period - 14 to 26 weeks (to 52 weeks if 2+ offences).
- Overall custody period - 14 to 45 days (to 90 days if 2+ offences).

- Monday to Thursday (4 days): Tuesday to Friday (4 days): Friday evening to Sunday (3 days) depending upon individual circumstances.

8.31.2. Suspended sentence

The custody criteria must be met. A suspended sentence sets the period of custody to be served if the order is not complied with. The court may order the offender to comply with one or more requirements as described above for community orders. The requirements exist within the 'supervision period'. The order is that the imprisonment does not take effect unless the offender fails to comply with a requirement or commits an offence during the 'operational period'.

The period of custody must be exactly the same as if it had been imposed forthwith. It cannot be longer simply because it may not happen. It is arguable that the imposition of a suspended sentence is 'pure punishment' and any requirements would be expected to deal with rehabilitation and protection, i.e. supervision is the likeliest requirement, whereas a high unpaid work requirement could potentially overload the punishment. The SGC state that 'Because of the very clear deterrent threat involved in a suspended sentence, requirements imposed as part of that sentence should generally be less onerous than those imposed as part of a community sentence. A court wishing to impose onerous or intensive requirements should reconsider its decision to suspend sentence and consider whether a community sentence might be more appropriate.'

Periodic court reviews at specified intervals may be imposed (except for a Drug Rehabilitation Requirement which carries its own specific review provision).

- 14 days to 26 weeks for one or more offences (transitional limit until custody plus is implemented and the increase of Magistrates' Court powers when the period will be 28 weeks to 51 weeks)
- 'Supervision period' of 6 months to 2 years (cannot end later than operational period)
- 'Operational period' of 6 months to 2 years (SGC guideline - operational period of up to 12 months for sentences of up to 6 months)

Example:

A period of 16 weeks imprisonment suspended for 12 months with a supervision requirement for 6 months. The operational period is 12 months. The supervision period is 6 months.

8.31.3. Breach of suspended sentence

The offender is warned or breached on the first failure to comply with a community requirement, and must always be breached on a second failure within 12 months. The options on breach are listed below, and they also apply to the commission of a further offence during the operational period.

- Activate the suspended sentence with the original term of custody unaltered, e.g. imposition of the 16 weeks custody forthwith.
- Reduce the original custodial period, e.g. reduction from 16 weeks to 4 weeks custody forthwith as the requirements have been complied with in full and the new offence is of a different nature.
- Amend the requirements to be more onerous, e.g. addition of a curfew requirement for 3 months as there has been substantial progress with the supervision in spite of the breach.
- Extension of the supervision period or operational period, e.g. extension of operational period from 12 months to 18 months as the new offence has occurred within the final month of the operational period.

The court must activate the imprisonment on breach of requirement or commission of further offence unless it would be 'unjust' to do so in view of the circumstances, and reasons must be given. Consideration must be given to the extent of compliance with the requirement(s) and the facts of the subsequent offence. The reality of breach for a regular drug user is very high, particularly in the first weeks of treatment. The court may consider that a high community order with the benefit of DRR, supervision and a programme may be more appropriate as such, with the clear stipulation that it is sentenced in the 'so serious' band. Custody would then be available but only after wilful and persistent failure, rather than as a start point for a first breach. The requirements may be amended in the same way as a community order, e.g. cancelling/replacing.

8.31.4. Case law guidance on imposition of custodial sentences

R v. Kefford 2002

The Lord Chief Justice, Lord Woolf said:

'Nothing that we say in this judgement is intended to deter courts from sending to prison for the appropriate period those who commit offences involving <u>violence or intimidation or other grave crimes</u>. Offences of this nature, particularly if they are committed against vulnerable members of the community undermine the public's sense of safety and the courts must play their part in protecting the public from these categories of offences. There are, however, other categories of offences where a community punishment or a fine can be sometimes a more appropriate form of sentence than imprisonment'.

In the case of economic crimes, for example, obtaining undue credit by fraud, prison is not necessarily the only appropriate form of punishment. Particularly in the case of those who have no record of previous offending, the very fact of having to appear before a court can be a significant punishment. Certainly, having to perform a form of community punishment can be a very salutary way of making it clear that crime does not pay, particularly if a community punishment order is combined with a curfew order'.

8.32. Committal for sentence

The following offences are examples of 'Committal to Crown Court' entry points in the Sentencing Guidelines:

Burglary of dwelling; Supply of drugs - all classes; Racially or religiously aggravated assault occasioning actual bodily harm; Violent disorder; Wounding - grievous bodily harm.

Effectively the guideline is stating that the offence is likely to merit more than 6 months imprisonment and would therefore be beyond the powers of the Magistrates' Court.

It is important to be particularly vigilant about the limitation of sentencing powers in these types of cases so that they are properly committed to Crown Court for sentence if appropriate at the earliest opportunity. In most cases this can be identified after the prosecution outline e.g. serious domestic burglary.

Discussion should always take place on the bench as to appropriate venue where the entry point is committal, particularly before adjourning for pre-sentence reports. The defence must be allowed to address the court following the bench's indication that it is minded to commit to Crown Court. There may be sufficient mitigation to bring the case down to Magistrates' Court powers. In such cases it is important to consider adding a rider to any adjournment for pre-sentence reports so that the next bench may commit the case to the Crown Court. If the rider is not added, the court has effectively given a binding indication that the maximum penalty will be 6 months imprisonment. If the next bench were to disagree and commit, the Crown Court will struggle to justify a longer penalty after that indication has been given, unless there is new information.

The National Mode of Trial guidelines (section 2 of Adult Court Bench Book), provide helpful indicators of aggravating features for specific offences which assist in the determination of whether a case lies outside the magistrates' powers. This may occur at the point of considering committal for trial or at consideration of committal for sentence.

Example:

> Adult Bench Book 2.8. Dangerous driving. Entry = Custody.
>
> Consider Committal to Crown Court if one or more of the following features are present and sentencing powers are insufficient:
>
> 1. Alcohol or drugs contributing to the dangerous driving
> 2. Grossly excessive speed
> 3. Racing
> 4. Prolonged course of dangerous driving
> 5. Significant injury or damage sustained
> 6. Other related offences.

8.33. Deferred sentence

The court may defer sentence for the purpose of enabling the sentencing court to have regard to the offender's conduct after conviction (including the making of reparation and compliance with any requirements) or any change of circumstances (schedule 23).

- The offender must consent and 'undertake' to comply with any requirements as to his conduct during the period of the deferment that the court considers appropriate e.g. attendance at an alcoholics' help group and payment of compensation voluntarily.
- It must be in the interests of justice to defer, having regard to the nature of the offence and the character and circumstances of the offender.
- A further offence or a failure to comply with a requirement brings forward the deferral and sentence may be imposed immediately.

Example:

The offence of assault is alcohol-related. The court believes that the offender has demonstrated commitment to address the problem by attending a help group for the last 6 weeks since the offence occurred. The purpose of rehabilitation is a realistic prospect by continuing to engage with the group for the next 6 months.

There is a wide scope to the potential requirements, or 'undertakings'. They may include residence of the offender during the whole or part of the period, any of the community order requirements, and most usefully, any other undertaking as to behaviour which is outside of the normal sentencing menu. The court may appoint a probation officer or other appropriate person to act as supervisor to him with their consent, e.g. manager of voluntary schemes. The supervisor will monitor compliance with the requirements and provide information as to compliance at the time sentence, e.g. extent of attendance and any measurable progress. If the court is satisfied that the offender has failed to comply with one or more requirements, he may be brought back before the court and sentenced. The early sentence on breach of a requirement is new. No waiting until the end of the deferred period.

There is no provision to remand the offender during the period. The date and time are given at the time of deferring sentence, and if he does not attend on that date, then a summons or warrant if does not attend on date given.

If a further offence is committed during the period then the court has power to sentence both for the original and the new offence at once.

The benefit of a deferred sentence is that measurable commitments can be tested outside of a court sentence alongside the threat of immediate sentence if the commitment falters or there is a further offence. It is expected to apply only to a small group where the offender is close to a particular type of sentence, usually custody. The expectation is that if he complies with the requirements, then the sentence would reduce from 'so serious' custody to 'serious enough' community order or fine, or from community order down to fine.

The court should make it clear what type of sentence it would be minded to impose if the period is completed e.g. fine or discharge, so that there is an incentive to respond and clarity for the sentencing bench (SGC).

- ⏲ Up to 6 months maximum and cannot be further deferred.

ANCILLARY ('ADD ON') ORDERS

Effective sentencing may well require more than one order. Usually, both the defence and the probation report will point towards a single 'main' sentence - not necessarily the same one! It would hardly be expected that a defence advocate will suggest that his client also receives a further ancillary penalty, e.g. that he should be excluded from his local pub as well as being given a community order! Many of the penalties below can be made on the court's own initiative, and if not, some would seldom be made at all. They are largely victim-orientated and may satisfy the purpose of protection of the public far more effectively than the principal sentence. Magistrates will be more familiar with some than others, because some may also be made alone on a specific application to the court, e.g. local authorities regularly apply for ASBOs as a civil application. It cannot be emphasised enough that they may also be added on to a criminal sentence. It is simply a question of inviting representations from the advocates if the court is minded to impose the addition, and then possibly reducing the main sentence so that overall there is a proportionate restriction on liberty.

8.34. Anti-Social Behaviour Order (ASBO) or Criminal ASBO (CRASBO) or 'bolt-on' ASBO if made in criminal proceedings

There are two separate routes to the making of an ASBO:
- Following a specific civil application on complaint by a relevant authority, i.e. local authority, police, British Transport Police or registered social landlord (ASBO) or
- Following conviction for a criminal offence, it may be added to any sentence or to a conditional discharge (sometimes distinguished as a 'CR'ASBO).

The criteria is that the defendant has acted in a manner that caused or was likely to cause harassment, alarm or distress to one or more persons not of the same household as himself <u>and</u> that the order is necessary to protect relevant persons from further anti-social behaviour by him.

The order contains 'must not' prohibition(s). For example, 'must not associate in a public place with X'.; 'must not carry paint aerosol in a public place'; 'must not go within 100 metres of Y street as shown in blue on the map'.

If anything is done in breach of the order without reasonable excuse, it is an 'either-way' offence and carries 5 years custody at the Crown Court. The

==Sentencing Guideline entry point is custody.== Given the potential seriousness of outcome, the breach must be proved beyond reasonable doubt. The defendant or relevant authority may apply for variation and discharge but the consent of the relevant authority is required for early discharge of a minimum 2 year order.

The prohibitions must be specific and relate to the situation described to the court. They cannot be imposed simply to increase the punishment for the behaviour. For example, 'must not drive whilst disqualified'. is also an offence which carries 6 months imprisonment and it should not be included as a prohibition simply to increase the potential penalty to 5 years imprisonment for a breach of the order.

Both an ASBO and CRASBO may now be made as an interim order if it is just to do so and further information is required before a full order can be made (July 2005). In many circumstances an Acceptable Behaviour Contract (ABC) precedes court action. This usually involves the police and/or local authority who will agree terms of conduct on a similar basis to a court ASBO, but possibly with positive actions as well. For example, an ABC with a 'kerb crawler', 'must not enter X (red light area) and must attend a briefing session about the dangers caused by prostitution'. The threat is that if it is not complied with, then an application for a court ASBO with court sanctions is likely to be applied for.

As a civil application, the adult court deals with applications in respect of children aged 10 and above, because the youth court does not have jurisdiction for civil matters - only criminal. Additionally the court must also consider making a parenting order on the parent (see 8.40) and reporting restrictions must be considered (see 7.5.3).

- Breach - an either-way offence - up to 5 years custody at Crown Court
- Not less than 2 years. No maximum.
- Effective from the day it is made, but may suspend requirements during period in custody e.g. not to contact co-accused prohibition is suspended whilst serving custodial sentence as both may be committed to the same custodial institution.

8.34.1. Individual Support Order (ISO)

If an ASBO is made in respect of a youth, the court must consider whether an Individual Support Order is desirable to prevent any repetition of the behaviour which led to the order being made. If so, the youth must comply with the requirements as specified and comply with the directions of the responsible officer for up to 6 months. The requirements may include activities, reporting or compliance with education arrangements. A report must be obtained from the local authority or youth offending team so that appropriate requirements can be considered.

- Breach: Age 10-13 = £250. Age 14-17 = £1,000
- Up to 6 months maximum or earlier if ASBO ceases to have effect.

8.35. Sexual Offences Prevention Order (SOPO)

There are three separate routes to the making of a SOPO:

- Following a specific civil application on complaint by the police if the offender has been convicted in the past of relevant sexual offence(s) and he has since acted in such a way as to give reasonable cause to believe that it is necessary for such an order to be made.
- Following conviction for a specified sexual offence, e.g. rape, intercourse with girl under 13, intercourse with a girl under 16 if the offender was aged 20 or more.
- Offender is under a disability and has done the act as charged above.

The criteria is that the court is satisfied that it is necessary to make such an order, for the purpose of protecting the public or any particular members of the public from serious sexual harm from the defendant.

Like an ASBO, it contains prohibitions. For example, 'not to go within 500 metres of any school'; 'not to attend public swimming baths during weekends and school holidays'; 'not to enter a public park after dusk (hours as defined in annexe)'. The order may be made as an interim order, and may be varied or discharged.

- ❑ Breach - an either way offence - up to 5 years custody at Crown Court
- ⏲ Period of not less than 5 years as specified, or until further order.

8.36. Other orders associated with sexual offences

- **Notification/Registration requirements**

Arising from conviction for specified sexual offences, the offender is required to notify the police of his name/address/national insurance details within 3 days of conviction. Any change of address must thereafter be notified for the period of registration, e.g. 5 years registration if a community order is made. Note that in a few cases the requirement depends upon the outcome at sentence. For example, sexual assault depends upon whether there is a sentence of imprisonment or a community sentence of at least 12 months. Failure to comply with the requirements carries a maximum of 5 years imprisonment. In May 2005 there were 1760 registered sex offenders in West Yorkshire.

When dealing with any sexual offences it is well worth checking with the legal adviser whether registration is required on conviction, especially if the case is subsequently adjourned for reports or committed for sentence, and also pausing to consider whether a SOPO is necessary at the point of sentence. We're grateful for the prompt!

- **Notification/Risk of Sexual Harm/Foreign Travel Order**

There are also a number of specific applications which may be made by the police. Application for a Notification Order if the conviction was overseas; a Risk of Sexual Harm Order where the behaviour falls short of a criminal offence, and a Foreign Travel Order if there is evidence that a sex offender intends to commit offences against children abroad.

8.37. Bind over

The order can be made on specific application e.g. prosecution application when a charge is to be withdrawn or as an ancillary penalty following conviction, e.g. Community Order and a bind over for a domestic assault.

The criterion is that the court has grounds for believing that there is a risk of a future breach of the peace. This is based upon the circumstances of the offence e.g. the words spoken indicate that the problem may recur, and/or any relevant previous convictions for disorder.

The order is to enter into a recognisance in terms chosen by the court as to duration and amount e.g. 'bind over to keep the peace for 12 months in the sum of £500'. All or part of which may be forfeited if the bind over is breached. Means information is therefore required. In order to ensure clarity and certainty under the Human Rights Act, it is important to specify the behaviour which will be punished on breach, so far as it can be defined. For example, to 'keep the peace' and/or 'to be of good behaviour and in particular not to assault/molest/interfere with XX .... or repeat the type of behaviour we have just heard about, namely ... (JCS and MA guidance 2000).

Refusal to enter into the recognisance may result in imprisonment up to 6 months (defendants over 21 only), or up to the point of agreement to enter the recognisance, if the order is made upon complaint. However, consent is not required if the order is made as an ancillary penalty to a criminal sentence. Simply seek representations and then make the order (R v. Crown Court at Lincoln ex.p Jude 1997).

This is a valuable order and should arguably be considered on the court's own initiative whenever dealing with offences of violence and disorder as a protective and deterrent element. It is also a helpful indicator on the record for the police, especially in domestic violence cases. The defendant must always be given the opportunity to make representations if the court indicates that it is minded to add a bind over.

- ❑ Breach - forfeiture of all, or part, or none, of the fixed amount
- ⊕ No maximum or minimum periods
- ⊕ No maximum amount, but it should reflect the means of the individual and the type of behaviour it is intended to deter. 'Drunk and disorderly' behaviour should arguably reflect the band A fine guidance for the offence if convicted, whilst an assault, carrying fear of future violence could justify an amount which would extend to the full 12 month repayment period if forfeited in full.

8.38. Exclusion Order (licensed premises)

The criterion is that there is a conviction for an offence on licensed premises and in committing the offence, the defendant resorted to violence or threatened to do so. It prohibits the defendant from entering specified licensed premises without the licensee's consent, but he may permit entry, e.g. if his profits slump during the exclusion! The order may extend to other specified licensed premises if considered necessary, e.g. the public house across the road.

The licensee may expel a defendant who enters in breach of an exclusion order and the police must help on request. This is a court order and is far stronger than simply relying upon doormen and local bans which are not enforceable in court, and when police intervention is only warranted when the trouble has actually happened.

- ❑ Breach penalty = level 3 fine/1 month imprisonment
- ⊕ Minimum = 3 months. Maximum = 2 years.

8.39. Football banning order

This is basically a 'stay away' order. There are two routes to the making of a football banning order:

- The offender is convicted of a 'relevant offence' e.g. vandalism in the ground, threats of violence on the journey to the match. This is the usual route and it will be attached as an ancillary order to the main penalty, e.g. Community Order + football banning order.
Or
- By application on complaint if the court is satisfied that the respondent has at any time caused or contributed to any violence or disorder in the UK or elsewhere. 'Violence' may be against persons or property, and includes threatening violence. It need not necessarily be in connection with football.

The criterion is that the court has reasonable grounds to believe that a banning order will help to prevent violence or disorder at or in connection with any regulated football matches. Reasons must be given if an order is not made.

The order prohibits the subject from entering a football ground to attend a 'regulated match' e.g. Premier League, Football League, UEFA Cup. He must report to a specified police station within 5 days of the order (unless in custody). A requirement may be included for his photograph to be taken by the police.

He must surrender his passport when regulated matches are played outside the UK unless there are exceptional reasons for not doing so e.g. pre-booked business trip. The order may be varied on application, and application for early termination may be made two-thirds of the way through the order.

- ❑ Breach penalty = 6 months/£5,000
- ⊕ Criminal order following conviction: Minimum = 3 years. Maximum = 5 years, but 6 years to 10 years if custodial sentence imposed. Note that the minimum period is for 3 years – consider 'proportionality' of the order for a minor offence if there is also mitigation.
- ⊕ Order made on complaint: Minimum = 2 years. Maximum of 3 years.

8.40. Parenting Order

This is available as an ancillary penalty on a parent in four scenarios:

- A child or young person is convicted of a criminal offence
- An Anti-Social Behaviour Order is made on the child
- A Sexual Offences Prevention Order is made on the child
- Parent is convicted of failing to ensure school attendance

The criterion is that the order is considered to be desirable to prevent repetition of the behaviour which led to order, or the commission of a further offence.

The parent is required to comply with such requirements as are specified in the order for up to 12 months <u>and</u> also attend guidance/counselling programme for up to 3 months as specified by the responsible officer, unless they have previously attended. The programme will be tailored to the individual. It may well be a couple of sessions, a weekly parent craft course over several weeks, or even a residential course.

Example: Failure to ensure school attendance

Requirement - Parent to comply with directions of education welfare officer and take all reasonable steps to ensure that child, Y, attends school for the next 12 months, commencing on .....

<u>And</u> *to attend 3 guidance/counselling sessions at .... on ..... and .... and ...*

The order must be explained to the parent, along with the proposed requirements. Application may be made for discharge or variation.

- ❑ Breach = level 3 fine (£1000)
- ⏱ Requirements up to 12 months
- ⏱ Sessions up to 3 months.

8.41. Restraining order

This ancillary order may be made when an offender is convicted of an offence contrary to the Protection from Harassment Act 1997 – causing harassment to another (s.2) or the more serious offence of conduct causing fear of violence (s.4). The order is designed to protect the victim from further harassment or fear of violence.

The terms may be similar to a bail condition and may contain specific exclusions and restrictions e.g. not to approach or communicate in any way with X, not to use 3rd parties to communicate with X, not to go within half a mile of X's home or place of work. The order may subsequently be varied or discharged.

- ❑ Breach = 6 months/£5,000 or 5 years/fine at Crown Court. If breach is in conjunction with a new offence, consider committal to Crown Court for sentence (R v Liddle 1999).
- ⏱ No maximum or minimum order. 'Until further order' may be appropriate.

8.42. Compensation

The order may be made as a penalty in its own right, or ancillary to another penalty. See 8.10.

Always consider – is there a specific victim? Is there evidence that they have suffered any damage, loss or injury, or terror and distress? Reasons are required if an order is not made.

- ⏲ Up to £5,000

8.43. Deprivation/Forfeiture Order

An order for deprivation or forfeiture may be made following conviction. This is when any lawfully seized property is in the defendant's possession or control when apprehended, and the item has been used to commit an offence, or it was intended to be used. For example, a jemmy or stolen credit card, or the offence consists of unlawful possession e.g. illegal drugs.

The court must have regard to the value, likely financial and other effect on defendant, and an order should only be made in cases where it will not be difficult to implement. The property is placed in police possession and subsequent application for possession may be made, The court does not determine ownership on making the order.

8.44. Prosecution costs on conviction

This is a normal ancillary order in most cases following conviction. The amount must be specified and the court must determine a 'just and reasonable' amount. It may include the costs of investigation as well as legal costs. The prosecution must serve on the defence, full details of the costs, in order to give a proper opportunity to consider and make representations.

If the defendant has the means to pay it is not wrong in principle to make an order for costs which exceed the amount of the fine, but the amounts should not be grossly disproportionate e.g. costs are in the thousands and fine is in the hundreds.

It is unlawful to make an order which the defendant has no realistic prospect of paying or in the hope that it will be paid by a 3rd party. Costs are recoverable in the same way as a fine, e.g. by attachment of benefits. Costs cannot be remitted as such, but may be written off with the consent of the prosecutor (blanket agreements exist up to limits, e.g. £100), or, otherwise a notional one day detention may be required.

- ⏲ Normal maximum repayment period = 12 months.

TRAFFIC PENALTIES

8.45. Endorsement and penalty points

Endorsement is obligatory for specified offences e.g. failing to comply with a red traffic light, using a vehicle without insurance, speeding, unless there is disqualification instead. The only exception to mandatory endorsement or disqualification is when special reasons apply (see 8.48). Every endorseable offence carries penalty points, whether fixed e.g. 3 penalty points for failing to comply with a red traffic light, or variable e.g. 6-8 for no insurance, 3-6 for speeding. The more serious the offence, the higher the points where there is a variable range. Details are endorsed on the driving licence (if held) and also recorded at Driver and Vehicle Licensing Authority (DVLA) at Swansea. The DVLA record can be accessed by the courts and is produced as a computer 'print-out' for court reference.

Where there are 2 or more offences on the same occasion, statute says that 'the total number of penalty points to be attributed to them is the number or highest number that would be attributed to the offence ...', but .. 'the court may if it thinks fit determine' that this does not apply and reasons must be given.

Example: The 'norm'

Date of offence	Offence	Points available	Final decision
1.8.05	No insurance	Variable 6-8	8 POINTS
1.8.05	Drive other than in accordance with provisional licence i.e. no 'L' plates or qualified passenger	Fixed 3	No points awarded as the insurance carries the higher.

The provision regarding allocation of separate points is rarely used. This is because where the scenario exists to distinguish the offences as being worthy of separate allocation, the reality is that the court will most likely be considering a short discretionary disqualification.

Example: The 'exception'

Date of offence	Offence	Points available	Final decision
1.8.05	No insurance	Variable 6-8	8 POINTS
1.8.05	Speeding	Variable 3-6	3 POINTS

Reasons for awarding separate points - offences are entirely different types of offences which require a different type of culpability - a document offence, and a driving offence - this is marked by awarding points on all matters.

Reality? The first consideration would be to order a discretionary disqualification as the speeding aggravates the more serious offence of no insurance.

Points remain physically on the driving licence for 4 years, except for alcohol related offences which remain for 11 years. This is because points are valid for 3 years for the purpose of points disqualification and for 10 years in respect of increased alcohol related disqualification.

8.46. Disqualification

This is an immediate order and disqualifies the defendant from driving any motor vehicle on a public road. The Sentencing Guidelines entry point for driving whilst disqualified is a community penalty and the offence carries imprisonment. The minimum period is fixed for the mandatory disqualification offences and for the 'points' disqualification. The maximum period in all cases is 'life' disqualification if appropriate, but it is accepted that generally there should be 'light at the end of the tunnel' and lengthy periods may be counter-productive, particularly for the young offender. It is available as an ancillary penalty and additionally, from January 2004 disqualification became available as a penalty in its own right in respect of any offence, including non-motoring offences.

- **Mandatory disqualification**

A minimum period of 12 months disqualification applies to the following offences unless special reasons apply: -

    (i) Driving or attempting to drive whilst unfit through drink/drugs
    (ii) Driving or attempting to drive with excess alcohol
    (iii) Driving and failing to provide a specimen without reasonable excuse
    (iv) Dangerous driving
    (v) Aggravated taking without consent (even the passenger!),

In respect of offences (i)(ii)(iii) the period of 12 months is increased to 3 years if the offender has already been convicted within the past 10 years. It is increased to 2 years if the offender has been disqualified for 56 days or more on 2 or more occasions in the 3 years preceding the offence. This may sound complicated but the legal adviser will draw this to your attention as necessary, but it is well worth being broadly aware that the minimum mandatory periods can increase if there is a previous disqualification, and we are grateful for your prompt!

It is not possible to reduce a mandatory disqualification period on the basis that there is substantial mitigation e.g. the defendant drank a relatively small amount of alcohol on the night before, had very little to eat, and honestly believed that he would no longer be over the prescribed limit. The only exception is when special reasons are successfully argued (See 8.48).

The disqualification period for the alcohol-related offences may however be reduced if the offender satisfactorily completes a specified approved course under the Drink Drive Rehabilitation Scheme (DDRS). The reduced period is not less than 3 months and cannot exceed one quarter of the unreduced period e.g. a 12 month ban may be reduced to 9 months. The course fee is income-related and is payable by the defendant to the course organiser, rather than the court. Consent is required on the day of sentence and the full period and potential reduced period are announced. Appropriate warnings must be given that the course fee must be paid <u>and</u> the course must be satisfactorily completed at least 2 calendar months prior to the end of the disqualification if the reduced period is to be effective. In West Yorkshire around one half of the defendants who say that they intend to do the course, actually do pay the fee and complete the course.

- **Discretionary disqualification**

A discretionary disqualification may be imposed for any endorseable offence, and also for taking a motor vehicle without consent (although not endorseable). Basically, it is saying that the offence is 'too serious for mere points - off the road!' There is no lower or upper limit to a discretionary disqualification.

Examples:

1. The Sentencing Guidelines give an entry point of discretionary disqualification of up to 56 days for driving at a speed over 101 mph in a 70 mph area or over 51 mph in a 30 mph area.

2. Speeding and driving without insurance as a combination - 8 points + 3 points may not reflect the seriousness on the facts - 2 months disqualification.

3. A serious case of driving without due care and attention - the 9 point maximum points does not reflect the seriousness of the case - 6 months disqualification + re-test (see below).

Any previous points will continue to be taken into account for 3 years for the purpose of a 'points disqualification' (see below). A discretionary disqualification does not wipe the slate clean of points - only a 'points disqualification' does that.

Always seek representations before imposing a discretionary disqualification.

- **'Points' disqualification (also known as 'totting')**

When 12 penalty points are accumulated by offences committed within the 3 year period, before or after the current offence, the court must disqualify for a minimum of 6 months unless 'exceptional hardship' is proved. The minimum of 6 months is increased to 12 months if there has been 1 other disqualification of <u>56 days or more</u> within the 3 year period, and to 2 years if there has been 2 such disqualification periods. There is no need to memorise the periods, but please check the relevant period with the legal adviser whenever there is a previous disqualification. Any 'points disqualification' wipes the slate clean of points, but not disqualification.

It is desirable to hear sworn evidence as to any plea of 'exceptional hardship'. This is about the particular defendant before the court and his personal circumstances. It is not about the offence - no matter how trivial it is - the endorsement and appropriate points must be applied.

The court may decide either not to disqualify at all or may reduce the period if satisfied that there is 'exceptional hardship' e.g. reduction from 6 months to 28 days disqualification (points are cleared), or no disqualification at all (points remain). 'Exceptional' hardship is a greater burden than simply proving hardship which is virtually inevitable to some extent for every defendant.

Example:

Questions regarding potential loss of employment will normally include:

- What exactly is the job and what does the job description require in respect of driving?
- When exactly does the defendant have to drive in his employment?
- Could anyone else drive instead?
- What inconvenience/cost would this actually create?
- May the defendant be moved to a non-driving role for a period of time?
- How long has he been employed in the current driving role?
- What other skills does he have for employment?
- What is his current wage?
- What would the alternative income be in different employment, or on state benefit (when eligible)?
- Is there satisfactory proof that the defendant would actually be dismissed if the licence is lost?

It will usually be necessary for the defendant to produce written evidence that he requires a driving licence to continue his employment e.g. contract, letter from employer, along with details of his current financial situation. Similarly evidence should be sought to prove that any onerous family transport responsibilities must inevitably fall upon the defendant. Alternative employment arrangements and alternative modes of transport should be explored. It is relevant that the hardship may well fall upon the defendant's family or employees.

The same reason cannot be put forward for 'exceptional hardship' if a further offence is committed during the 3 year period. It may well be that a 'delayed' ban would justifiably be for more than the 6 month minimum as the points would obviously have gone higher than 12.

- **Discretionary disqualification or 'points disqualification?**

In many situations the latest offence may be serious enough to merit a discretionary disqualification, but there may be existing points which mean that a points ban would apply if points only were imposed. It is now permissible to consider a discretionary disqualification 'in parallel' with the possibility of imposing points and reaching a 'points disqualification' situation (Jones v. Chief Constable of West Mercia 2000). However, the nature of the record must be carefully considered before imposing a short discretionary disqualification for the current offence.

The two scenarios are quite dramatically different and the 'pros and cons' need to be weighed. Take an offence of speeding. A discretionary disqualification for 42 days for the isolated offence of high speeding is very different to endorsing the licence and awarding 6 points which take the defendant into a 'points disqualification' of 6 months.

What is the court trying to achieve with this defendant - punishment or deterrence? By imposing the discretionary disqualification, on the one hand, he will lose his licence for only 42 days but with the 6 previous points remaining intact as a warning. Alternatively, by imposing a points disqualification, he will lose his licence for the full 6 months but the pre-existing 6 points will be wiped clear. Not an easy decision!

It is important to recognise the benefit to the defendant of reducing a points disqualification down to 7 days on the basis of exceptional hardship - 7 days and then a clear licence and no mandatory increase if the 12 points accrue again!

Remember that the 6 months increases to 12 months 'points disqualification' <u>if</u> there is a previous disqualification of <u>56 days or more</u> in the last 3 years.

Watch out for the disqualification periods of 56 days or more in the last 3 years as they are just as important as penalty points for the calculation of the current disqualification period.

- **Interim disqualification**

Disqualification may be ordered on an interim basis when a case is adjourned following conviction. For example, adjournment for pre-sentence reports; committal to Crown Court for sentence; remittal to another Magistrates' Court, or being subjected to deferment of sentence. The disqualification will lapse if the defendant is not sentenced before the expiry of 6 months, and the one interim disqualification allowed, will usually be for '6 months or until the case is dealt with if sooner'. This will ensure that a disqualified defendant who fails to attend the next hearing, will at least be disqualified for up to 6 months, unless he is arrested in the meantime.

The final disqualification will take into account the interim period e.g. an obligatory 12 month disqualification will effectively be back-dated to the commencement of the interim ban. This is a useful power which ensures that the public are protected immediately, albeit there are further issues to pursue before final sentence.

- **Disqualification until test is passed (must comply with provisional licence requirements during disqualification period)**

This disqualification usually follows on after a full disqualification, but may be imposed as a penalty alone. It enables the defendant to drive, but he must comply with full provisional licence requirements, whether he has ever passed a test or not. Otherwise he is committing the offence of driving whilst disqualified. Effectively he is disqualified from driving unless he has 'L' plates and a qualified passenger.

The court *must* disqualify an offender until he passes an extended driving test if he is convicted of dangerous driving. The court *may* disqualify until a test is passed in any case involving obligatory endorsement if there is concern about the 'safety of other road users' e.g. serious careless driving; record of 'bad driving'; lengthy disqualification so that driving skills will be stale. The extended test will apply if the defendant is convicted of an offence involving mandatory disqualification e.g. driving over the prescribed limit, or a points disqualification. The ordinary test applies to the remainder, e.g. discretionary disqualification for careless driving.

The question effectively is whether this defendant is safe on the road without 'L' plates and a qualified passenger. There may be concern by the bench that he will simply get back in a car and drive without any supervision or 'L' plate warning to others, following a serious incident, after the end of a long disqualification, or when he has never passed a test at all!

This is significant when the defendant has never passed a driving test as the order makes it far more serious than simply not complying with his provisional licence by driving without the 'L' plates and passenger - he is driving whilst disqualified under the test requirement provision. Although often referred to as the 're-test' provision it also applies to a first test. It may be an appropriate penalty for the repeated totter who has failed to respond to the first totting disqualification and goes on to do this again by driving without complying with the provisional licence requirements. He seems determined not to comply with provisional licence holder requirements. In such cases the penalty of another points disqualification and the extra responsibility when he returns to driving is likely to protect the public far more than a fine. The disqualification may be imposed as a penalty in its own right - previous fines may well remain to be paid.

The disqualification must be based upon the statutory provision, which is for the court to 'have regard to the safety of other road users'. It is not about creating additional punishment for driving without documents!

8.47. Revocation of licence by DVLA, Swansea

A new 'probationary' driver who has passed the relevant test e.g. motor cycle, motor car within the past 2 years and acquires 6 penalty points is subject to revocation of his full licence by the DVLA. Effectively he will revert to provisional licence status. Whilst this is not an order of the court, account should be taken of the implication. In binding case law, the sentencing court awarded 6 points and declared that it would not disqualify as the defendant lived in a rural area without regular buses and required a full licence to get to work. The Court of Appeal substituted 5 points as it was considered that the sentencing court had effectively disqualified him, by rendering him liable to revocation and the requirement to find a qualified passenger at all times (Re: Damien Edwards 2000).

8.48. Special reasons

Endorsement and/or disqualification may be avoided if the court is satisfied that a special reason exists. The main point is that the reason relates to the offence itself, rather than to the offender. All the offender mitigation in the world cannot avoid a mandatory disqualification. It is completely different from the 'exceptional hardship' argument when 12 points are reached, which relates to the offender. For special reasons to apply, the question is what was so special about this particular offence? The reason must satisfy 4 criteria:

(i) It must be a mitigating or extenuating circumstance about the offence
(ii) It does not constitute a legal defence e.g. that the defendant was not actually 'driving' the car, or the scene of the incident was not a 'road'
(iii) It must be directly connected to the offence e.g. emergency situation; soft drink had been laced by alcohol without the defendant's knowledge and he had driven 'innocently unaware' of the high alcohol level
(iv) It must be a factor which the court ought properly to take into consideration such as whether the defendant acted responsibly and reasonably e.g. was it appropriate to drive to the hospital in an intoxicated state rather than ringing for an ambulance or a taxi?

The court must then consider whether to exercise its discretion. This will depend upon various factors e.g. in what manner was the vehicle driven, the reason for the car being driven, level of danger to others, distance driven.

There are numerous cases involving special reasons and the legal adviser's advice should always be sought before making a determination in this complex area.

Example:

A frequent special reason put forward is 'shortness of distance driven.' Guidance has been given that the court must look not only at what the defendant had actually achieved but at what he intended. In the case concerned he fully intended to drive home and special reasons were not made out (CPS v. Dean Humphries 2000).

Traffic procedures

8.49. 'Speed camera offences'

A Notice of Intended Prosecution is sent to the registered keeper stating where and when the speeding vehicle has been 'captured' on camera. The keeper may then acknowledge that he was the driver and pay the conditional fixed penalty ticket for speeding within 28 days, and submit his driving licence for endorsement and 3 penalty points. Alternatively he may disclose the name and address of the driver on the occasion of the incident, and the driver will then be sent a Notice of Intended Prosecution and be given the opportunity to pay and submit his driving licence in the same way.

If the keeper fails to disclose the name and address of the driver, he is committing an offence and the Sentencing Guideline entry point is a band C fine and 3 penalty points.

8.50. Uncontested road traffic matters

Most summary traffic matters are dealt with by way of summons. The majority of defendants choose not to attend. They either enter a guilty plea by post based upon a summary of the prosecution facts which are sent to them, or alternatively the case can be proved without their response if full statements are sent to them at least 10 days before the hearing. The court will obtain a print out of the driver's record from DVLC Swansea in readiness for the case to proceed – with or without a licence in court. In the latter scenario it is open to the defendant to ask for the case to be re-opened for another court hearing if he did not receive the summons and statements e.g. he was on holiday or had moved from the address given to the officer at the time.

CHAPTER 9
ROLE OF THE LEGAL ADVISER, PRE-COURT BRIEFING AND POST-SITTING REVIEW

9.1. Role of the legal adviser - Practice Direction

The most straightforward way to describe the role of the legal adviser is to summarise the provisions of the relevant Practice Direction (Justices: Clerk to Court) 2000 as below.

The Justices' Clerk has the following responsibilities and powers, which are delegated to the legal advisers:

- To give advice on the following matters, whether or not the justices so request
    - Questions of law, and mixed law and fact
    - Matters of practice and procedure
    - Range of penalties available
    - Relevant decisions of superior courts or other guidelines
    - Other issues relevant to the matter
    - Appropriate decision-making structure
- To assist the court, where appropriate, as to the formulation of reasons and the recording of those reasons.
- To ask questions of witnesses and the parties in order to clarify the evidence and any issues in the case.
- To ensure that every case is conducted fairly.
- To play no part in making findings of fact but may assist the bench by reminding them of evidence, using any notes of the proceedings.
- To assist an unrepresented party to present his case, without becoming an advocate for the party.
- To be allowed in default proceedings, to ask questions to elicit information. The legal adviser must not appear to be adversarial or partisan. Advice may be given upon the various options, but he cannot set out to establish wilful refusal/culpable neglect, or offer opinion on facts, or urge a particular course of action on the bench.

The Direction also includes two procedural points:

- Any request by the bench for the legal adviser to join the bench in the retiring room should be made in open court, in the presence of the parties.
- Any advice given in the retiring room is 'provisional' and should be repeated for representations in open court and then the advice should be confirmed or varied openly.

9.1.2. Delegated powers

The Justices' Clerk may also authorise the legal adviser to deal with particular cases in the absence of a bench. For example, adjournment on the same bail as before with the consent of prosecution and defence; giving directions in relation to a trial; variation of fine instalments and making applications for attachments of benefits and earnings. These powers enable legal advisers to deal with adjournments, pre-trial reviews and some fine default cases without a bench.

9.1.3. Practical functions

Local practices vary slightly, but in practical (rather than legal), terms the legal adviser will normally deal with:

- Identification of the defendant and reading out the allegation
- Provision of information to the bench about the history of the case
- Liaison with the usher, prosecutor, defence solicitors and prison escort services to keep the list running smoothly
- Liaison with court listing officers to fix adjournment dates
- Completion of the paperwork e.g. results, notices to defendant (please allow time for this to happen!)
- Grant of legal representation orders
- 'Filling the gaps' in the proceedings.

9.2. Pre-court briefing

This is a short team meeting between the magistrates and the legal adviser before the court begins. It looks forward to what lies ahead and who will do what, so that the work is dealt with effectively and efficiently.

9.2.2. Content of the list

This is something beyond the enquiry "Is it a heavy list? What time can we expect to finish?" It is the opportunity to be prepared for the types of case which the bench will face and the kind of information you will need to hand.

Examples:

1. What type of list is it?
   Largely arrest warrants and bail applications and then a trial. It may be helpful to have the structured approaches to hand. Bail is at 1-21, and verdict is at 1-35 in the Bench Book.

2. Could you remind me if there are any new practices around bail - it's a long time since I sat in a remand court?
   Yes, when the defendant appears in custody after arrest on warrant, the expectation now is that the failure to surrender charge will be put to

him, and if it is a guilty plea, then he would normally be sentenced today. In the past, the bail charge was usually adjourned along with the original offence so that everything was dealt with together. The guideline entry point is for a community penalty and locally the starting point would be a 28 day curfew requirement.

3. Are there any multi-handed cases?
A 6-handed case which includes 2 youths who will be with parents - all separately represented. Perhaps you would like to mark them in advance on your list.

4. Are there any cases with a lengthy history which need to be expedited?
Yes, we have an application to adjourn to a 2nd trial date because of an absent witness. This is a copy of the pre-trial review form and the certificate of trial readiness for your reference. The case management structure has some useful adjournment questions listed at 1-15 in the Bench Book.

5. Are there any defendants or witnesses with special needs?
One of the witnesses is a wheelchair user. We've created some space next to the witness box so that he can give his evidence from there, and he's familiarised himself with the lay out.

6. This is my first time in chairing a trial - I'd like to try and manage it, but will you jump in if I miss anything and give me some feedback at the end of the court?

(N.B. Not all examples would be expected in a single list!)

9.2.3. Legal adviser - agree speaking roles

This may vary between various partnerships, depending upon individual strengths and preferences. There is no legal requirement about who says what and when. This avoids the danger of both the chairman and legal adviser speaking at once, or a defendant being faced with an intermittent barrage from both without any clear picture emerging about who is actually in charge of the court and making the decisions.

The five main areas for agreement are:

1. Who will identify and charge? If this is the legal adviser, it is helpful to ask the defendant to give his name and address 'to the magistrates' so that eye contact is directed to the bench from the beginning, and the defendant is encouraged to speak early in the case.

2. Who will put any breaches of conditional discharge to the defendant? Lest they be forgotten!

3. Who will explain the course of the proceedings to an unrepresented defendant? There is much to be said for the chairman dealing with this at least on guilty pleas. Some 'hand over' words from the legal adviser such as 'May the defendant be seated?' will make it clear that the legal

adviser has completed all matters relating to charge. If the chairman explains what is to happen, it also demonstrates who is actually in charge of the court and lifts eye contact and interaction to the chairman and the bench, rather than to the legal adviser. It also avoids overlooking the fact that the defendant remains standing until an advocate interjects to ask for permission for him to be seated. The chairman may wish to give that that permission either before or after giving the explanation.

4. Who will draw out the mitigation with the unrepresented defendants?
5. Who will conduct the means enquiry? Obviously this would not preclude the legal adviser or chairman asking supplementary questions to obtain a full picture. The one who is actively listening is more likely to identify the gaps than the one is asking.

9.2.4. Wingers - who is going to do what?

There are a number of functions to perform in a crime list and it is important for the chairman to indicate what he prefers to do for himself and what he would like the wingers to do. Individual wingers may also have preferences, depending on their strengths.

Examples:

1. Turning to the Sentencing Guidelines - this should never be done 'in readiness' during a trial!
2. Turning to the relevant Pronouncements - this is particularly helpful when several different orders are being made, e.g. fine and disqualification.
3. Assessment of net income figure and 'doing the maths' in relation to the relevant band, A, B, or C - especially when variations are involved e.g. speeding.
4. Completing the reasons form as they are agreed.

9.2.5. Practicalities on the day

Different types of list and different groups of three will usually call for some identification of how you will work together. Having identified that the list is essentially made up non-attendances on a TV licence list, it may be helpful to identify the norm penalty and then set the parameters for when this will apply before going into court. This will save checking with each winger on every case.

Wingers will welcome the invitation to prompt, and the chairman may wish to identify just how he would prefer to be alerted. The chairmen must be prepared for when this does happen. Saying, 'I am grateful to my colleague for reminding me that we also agreed that you will pay £60 costs' is a more dignified and open acknowledgement than unexplained nudges and rustling notes in mid-pronouncement.

9.2.6. New practices and options

The pre-court briefing is also the opportunity for the legal adviser to inform the bench about new practices and options, and also, to identify any current issues which the court is attempting to address. This will provide a useful basis and focus for the post-court review.

Information may include, for instance, information about a new specified activity requirement which has become available locally; a reminder to consider attachment of benefits or earnings on first default hearings rather than simply adjourning to pay, based upon recent statistics of outcomes.

And finally, before going into court, note the names of the prosecutor, legal adviser, usher, court probation officer and the routine adjournment dates e.g. the date in 3 weeks time for the standard reports cases.

9.3. Post-sitting review

MNTI 2 brings with it the introduction of a post-court review by the bench and legal adviser, to briefly review the work at the end of the session. The MNTI 2 Handbook describes the review as follows:

'The aim is to identify and acknowledge good practice, identify what could be improved on and how to do things better, and to emphasise learning from that court sitting.

'It is part of an ongoing process and intended to help us to focus on aspects of the relevant competence framework. Discussions should be kept as brief as possible and be led by the chairman and involve the legal adviser. The spirit should be one of open, frank and free exchange between the members of the bench and the legal adviser'.

'If an appraisal is taking place, the review gives everyone the opportunity to make comments openly and for the appraiser and appraisee to take these into account in their private session following the review'.

The most important features of a post sitting review are to ask questions, clarify uncertainties, make suggestions, reflect on performance (especially with new situations), and give feedback. It may be helpful to have the checklist of the MNTI competences readily available for reference in the retiring room. When a court is clearly going to run on to a late finish, it may sometimes be practical to conduct the review during a natural break during the latter part of the session, e.g. whilst awaiting solicitors. It should only last for 5 to 10 minutes maximum. Surely there is at least one good action or word in a court sitting which is worthy of meaningful compliment. The chance of it being repeated in another court on another day will increase if it is specifically approved.

Sometimes a training request may emerge. The 'identification of training needs' can sound like a daunting experience. The reality is that if we feel that there was a point when we lost the plot, or did not feel confident enough to contribute on a particular issue, then there is a 'right to ask' in the safe environment of the post sitting review. So often, a training need, is no more than asking for explanation or clarification. Two minutes may be sufficient.

It is helpful to the Bench Training and Development Committee (BTDC) if any unresolved or more detailed requests for guidance are conveyed in writing. There will be a form for this purpose in the retiring room. A magistrate may simply want short written clarification either personally, or so often, it is a topic which is well worth covering through the bench bulletin for everyone. Alternatively there may be a request to run a particular course. Suggestions from magistrates immediately after a real experience are excellent sources for the BTDC when deciding upon courses and topics for the future. For example, an unfamiliar application for an arrest warrant by an Immigration Officer may prompt a suggestion for more information about the work of the regional office and explanation of the asylum process.

Occasionally legal advisers may be perceived to give different advice. It is helpful for this to be pointed out at the time. Sometimes we simply have not been clear and it is a misunderstanding. Sometimes, as lawyers acting largely independently we may interpret the law or practices in a different way - that is the nature of law! It is helpful for everyone for issues to be identified so that a consistent line can be discussed and resolved amongst the legal advisers. Help us please.

Post sitting review - examples

1. **New experiences.** The chairman recognises that in his first trial he had not been prepared for the defendant choosing not to give evidence, and thanks the legal adviser for giving the appropriate warning. The wingers compliment the chairman on the clarity of the structured approach in the retiring room.

2. **New sentencing options.** The new specified activity was used. A winger asks whether it is possible to find out if the requirement is complied with.
   Action: Legal adviser asks probation team to give feedback to the named magistrates when the activity period ends, or at least, give completion rates in the next probation bulletin.

3. **New practices.** The new practice of 'sentence on the day of arrest' for failure to surrender to bail was applied, but all recognised that the local defence solicitors were surprised by the change from adjourning for sentence along with the main offence.
   Action: Legal adviser to make sure that it is mentioned at the next meeting with solicitors.

4. **Current bench action points.** Efforts to attach enforcement options to fine defaulters are congratulated by the legal adviser because all of

the defaulters, except one, left court with an attachment to benefits or earnings. A winger seeks clarification about why benefits could not be attached in a particular case and the legal adviser explains that deductions cannot be made from incapacity benefit.

5. **Specific request.** A winger asks for the next bench bulletin to cover how or whether fixed penalty tickets for being drunk and disorderly should be brought to the attention of the court as if they were previous convictions. A defendant was clearly taken aback when this happened. He pointed out that the ticket stated that payment was not an admission of guilt and it would not be recorded against him, otherwise he would have disputed it instead of just paying up.

6. **Specific question.** A winger says that a previous legal adviser had said that an ASBO could not be made in a 'domestic case', whereas an order was made in court today between former partners. Clarification was given that the order could not be made in respect of someone in the 'same household' and in reality this normally did exclude ASBOs from the normal domestic case. In the case concerned, the parties were separated so the order could be made.

7. **Specific feedback.** The chairman points out the benefit of the occasions when the legal adviser actually stood up and faced the bench when giving the case history because it was heard so much more easily than the occasion when he sat down and faced the court. The advice throughout the day had been very clear and helpful.

Not all in one post sitting review!

9.4. Effective feedback

The big question basically is 'How did we do?' This is a genuine open question which makes the warm statement of team effort. This compares to the anxious or hurried question of 'Do we need a post-sitting review?' This creates an expectation that the anticipated answer is 'no' and takes away the opportunity to question, comment or ask. The aim is to ensure that everyone recognises that the post-sitting review is a genuine opportunity for 'any comments?' One compliment about something is a good baseline - one minute for a feel good factor must be a good thing. Sometimes there may be more, and if feedback is to be given, there are a few basic aspects to consider.

The MNTI Handbook states that ' Any feedback given should be balanced, objective, clear and specific...' Constructive feedback is helpful. We rarely give specific compliments to each other. A vague 'well done' is pleasant and uplifting for the day, but a few more words of detail will help to reinforce good practice. It is made clear then what exactly was 'well done' and encouragement generates a real likelihood that it will be repeated again.

By the same token, we rarely give meaningful negative feedback. It can be uncomfortable to criticise. There is also the temptation at the end of a court list, that the court has finally ended and the same team may not come together for a long time, so it is easy to walk away. The post court review is a window both to compliment each other and to identify problems and perhaps even find some solutions or refer them on as appropriate.

Feedback is the entitlement of all members of the bench and the legal advisers. It is about comment on a level playing field. Sharing personal feelings rather than making judgements. Recognising that this is the time to ask each other for suggestions rather than telling someone else what to do. There are a few well-recognised rules of feedback.

- Be specific and give reasons. Focus on the actual behaviour.

What exactly is being reinforced as good behaviour? The tighter the issues at the pre-court briefing, the easier to be specific later e.g. exactly how many enforcement options were attached to default cases and if not, why not. Give some evidence for every comment. Say how you feel because that is the main reason for taking the trouble to give feedback - there is a personal effect.

- Comment specifically as a personal view and say why. Broad compliments are pleasant but mean very little unless it is clear what is appreciated and why, so that it happens again.

Examples:

1. From the chairman 'You were all brilliant today. In fact we made an excellent team. Well done!. Let's go. **X**

2. To the winger, 'Thank you for working out the weekly net income figures so quickly. We had a lot of fines to calculate today from monthly salaries, and we'd normally face long pauses to do it properly. Today I felt pleased that we were starting with accurate figures for everyone, and we got through a big list.' ✓

3. To the chairman, 'Although you said that you were nervous, it didn't show at all - very clear and authoritative. I thought you dealt with the application to adjourn the trial very well. Your questions made it clear that the court really does manage the case and it would be going ahead as planned if at all possible. To your credit, it did. ✓

- Own the opinion you are about to give. Start with '<u>I</u>' think/saw/feel' because this concedes the important inference that you may well be wrong!

- Avoid starting the comment with 'You are' or 'It was' .Such comments are likely to be heard as a factual, unequivocal judgement which is not the purpose of feedback to colleagues.

Examples:

1. *'It was far too long a pronouncement. There was no need for all that. He just turned off'.* **X**
   'I saw the defendant turn away as you were going through the evidence. I don't think he was listening when you actually told him what the sentence was'. ✓

2. *'You just ran the court with Bob. I could have been invisible'.* **X**
   'I noticed that you always turn to Bob first on the bench and then turned to me with the decision of the two of you. That would be the majority, so I felt there was nothing for me to contribute really. I suppose we all have a tendency to turn one way or the other, but I felt a bit of a spare part at times. ✓

- Encourage 'asking', rather than simply 'telling'.
- Make 'asking for help and advice' 'ok',

We all make mistakes and we often recognise them immediately. It is more dignified to be given the opportunity to put things right ourselves without being told to, or reflect for ourselves on how we might approach a situation differently. This avoids the temptation to go into defensive, rather than solving mode. Questions often generate the admission and acknowledgement that help is needed, without losing face. Few people feel comfortable about being faced with a barrage of unsolicited advice, but will respond positively if they are given a 'fault-free' invitation to ask.

Examples:

1. *We came very close to contempt proceedings in the assault case. What did you think about that case?*
2. *Was your understanding that you were required to go through all the evidence after a trial? I've seen it done in various ways so I wonder if we could ask for some guidance from the legal adviser about what is actually required?*
3. *Have you come across this situation before? No. Well, I can share a similar experience if you think it might help?*

9.5. Giving feedback on sensitive issues

Occasionally, a comment may be made during a court hearing which a magistrate or legal adviser has serious concerns about. This could range from a racist or sexist remark, to a comment which demonstrates prejudice or labelling against a section of the community, e.g. 'they're all on drugs on that estate'. Something needs to be said to demonstrate that this is not acceptable. To 'let remarks go' is to passively collude with discrimination. There may well be no malicious intent whatsoever. There may well be a genuine lack of awareness that the remark may be regarded as offensive. More worryingly there may well be no recognition that the sentiment expressed may be a symptom of a prejudice, which may find it's way into the decision-making process. Feedback is about trying to raise awareness and influence each other's future behaviour in a positive way.

As with any feedback it is important to express personal feelings, based on specifics, rather than judge the person who may well be genuinely unaware, and eager to put things right immediately. Always give them chance to do that, give the ladder to climb out, and, if it is resolved, move the conversation on to avoid embarrassment.

Example:

'You're thoughtless ...the expression 'queer' is homophobic'. **X**

'You used the word 'queer' when describing the last witness ...' I know that the word is often used, but especially in the court setting, I think it can sound as if gay people are not equal and somehow valued differently. Do you use the term 'gay' as well? Yes. Well I'd be more comfortable with that and I think that it's generally the more acceptable expression now.... I agree with what you say about the potential for his evidence to be biased in favour of his boyfriend. ✓

When generalisations are made, it may be appropriate to question the basis of the comment, rather than comment upon it.

Example:

'Stealing cars is a way of life on that estate - they're all at it'.

'What makes you say that?'
'Would that affect how you deal with this defendant?'

Another strategy is to simply repeat the comment back in a tone of mild surprise to check that it has been heard correctly. This may be quite sufficient, with a pause to allow for an immediate withdrawal. This strategy can be very effective and far easier than engaging in discussion. From the point of view of the maker of the statement, he may genuinely wish that he had not made the remark and this option allows the opportunity to make a short apology and move on quickly. If you feel uncomfortable about a comment say so.

9.6. Receiving feedback

Accept praise thankfully rather than being diffident. Let's make it happen more, rather than being embarrassed about it. If concerns are recognised, it is just as important to receive feedback in a constructive manner, in the spirit of general improvement. It may assist to 'get there first' and at the beginning of the court to ask for feedback at the end. This may be particularly helpful if there is an area of uncertainty e.g. a chairman dealing with his first trial, or making an effort to increase volume when making pronouncements. Similarly at the end, it is more comfortable for colleagues to give feedback based upon an invitation. For instance, 'I'd welcome some suggestions on how I could have dealt with the difficult defendant in a different way? I really felt that I was losing patience'.

Post-court reviews are about striving for general improvement in the way we behave - magistrates and legal advisers. Personalities cannot be changed. Behaviour can be changed but it is about someone choosing to do so and therefore seeing a good reason to do so. Not every piece of feedback will be eagerly taken on board and result in immediate transformation - some will, and that makes the process well worthwhile.

CHAPTER 10
YOUTH COURT

10.1. Differences between the youth court and the adult court

The most important difference is that the youth court must always have regard to the welfare of the child or young person and to the principal aim of the youth justice system which is to prevent offending. These are both statutory requirements. The purposes described for adults take second place to welfare and prevention which guide all bail and sentencing decisions. Other differences are listed below:

10.1.1. The court list

- The age group of defendants are 'children' (aged 10 - 13) and 'young persons' (aged 14 -17). In this chapter the expression 'youth' refers to the full age group.
- The court only deals with criminal offences. Civil matters involving youths are dealt with in the adult court. For example, applications for ASBOs by the local authority are made in the adult civil court, but criminal bolt-on ASBOs and all breaches are dealt with in the youth court. The adult court does have some limited powers to deal with youth criminal matters. These are, remand applications, joint charges with an adult, and the imposition of a referral order, fine and discharge if convicted in the adult court.

10.1.2. The court

- The bench must be specifically trained to deal with youth court matters and should include a man and a woman, unless due to unforeseen circumstances this is not possible and it would not be in the interests of justice to adjourn the cases.
- A parent/guardian or appropriate adult must accompany a youth aged between 10-15 in the youth court, and may be asked to accompany the 16 and 17 year olds.
- The court is not open to the general public and only limited categories of additional people may attend. These are, officers of the court, the advocates, witnesses and those 'directly concerned with the case', bona fide Press representatives, and 'such other persons as the court may specially authorise', e.g. trainee social workers. The youth court must be kept as separate as possible from the adult courts.
- Statutory reporting restrictions apply as a starting point. There cannot be any report which reveals the name, address, school, or any particulars likely to lead to the identification of the youth. Pictures of the youth are not allowed. The exceptions are details of a bolt-on ASBO (CRASBO) and

breaches of an ASBO which may be published unless specifically restricted. In all other cases an application may be made to lift the restrictions, rather than to impose restrictions which is the situation in adult court. The criteria for lifting restrictions are that it would avoid injustice to the youth, or if he is unlawfully at large following a serious charge, or if he has been found guilty of an offence and the court is satisfied that it is in the public interest to do so. Representations must always be sought before lifting restrictions and reporting must never be regarded as part of the punishment (See 7.5.3.).
- The court is supported by the youth offending team, known as the 'yot', rather than a probation team. The yot is a multi-agency team which includes at least one probation officer, social worker, police officer, and a health and education officer.
- The proceedings are far more informal and the aim is for the bench to engage with the parent and youth so that they can contribute fully to the proceedings.

10.1.3. The sentence

- 'Restorative justice' plays a major part in most sentences, e.g. personal apology or letter, victim awareness, community work.
- The generic community order is not available (anticipated April 2007). Existing community orders continue.
- A sentence of imprisonment cannot be imposed. Detention and Training Orders are imposed instead and they extend to 2 years rather than 6 months.
- Credit for a guilty plea cannot be expressed for some of the sentences which are for fixed periods, e.g. Action Plan Order is 3 months. A number of other sentences are rehabilitative rather than punitive and credit is not appropriate, e.g. 180 day programmes within a supervision order, and they should not be reduced.

10.2. Pre-court interventions - Fixed penalty ticket, Reprimand and Final Warning

Fixed penalty tickets may be given to youths for certain alleged offences, e.g. £80 for being drunk and disorderly. It is important to recognise that the ticket makes it clear that payment is not an admission of guilt and that the offence will not appear as a conviction on the police national computer and it should not therefore be treated as such by the court. The recipient may request a court hearing but this carries the risk of conviction, a higher penalty, and most significantly, a criminal record. If the ticket is not paid, then it is registered for enforcement as a fine in the youth court.

Cautions cannot be given to youths. Reprimands and Final Warnings are given instead. A Reprimand is based upon an admission of the offence and it may be notified and considered by the court in future. Reprimands are used for a first time minor offence e.g. theft up to a value of £100, possession of a class B drug, if the police consider that it would not be in the public interest to prosecute the offence. The youth offending team (yot) are notified and may support as appropriate following a Reprimand.

The final tier, before charge is a Final Warning which may be given for a more serious first time offence, or a second offence if it was more than 2 years ago. For example, theft over £100, possession of a class A drug. All offences are given a starting point gravity score and aggravating or mitigating features may adjust an entry point of Final Warning down to a Reprimand or up to a charge. A Final Warning is administered by a police officer in the presence of a parent/guardian or an 'appropriate adult'. The youth offending team are notified and they will assess and, if necessary, organise an individual change programme with a restorative element e.g. apology, community activity, counselling, improvement in school attendance. The court may subsequently be told about the level of co-operation of such a programme. When a Final Warning has been administered, the court may not give a conditional discharge within 2 years unless there are exceptional circumstances. The most serious offences will always be charged.

10.3. Role of parent/guardian

10.3.1. Attendance at court

The court must require a parent or guardian to attend in respect of a youth who is under the age of 16, and may require attendance if the youth is 16 or 17 unless it is unreasonable, e.g. mother is ill and a responsible relative attends. A summons or warrant may be issued to secure attendance.

10.3.2. Parental bind over

A parent/guardian of a youth aged 10 - 15 must be bound over to take proper care and exercise proper control over a convicted youth if it would be desirable in the interests of preventing the commission of further offences. Reasons must be given if the order is not made, e.g. the parent has taken all reasonable steps to control and the court does not foresee any further offending. The order becomes discretionary if the youth is aged 16 -17. Consent is required, but unreasonable refusal may result in fine up to £1000.

- ❑ Breach - may forfeit up to amount of bind over
- ⏱ Maximum sum of £1000
- ⏱ Maximum period of 3 years or to age 18.

10.3.3. Parenting order

A parenting order must be made following conviction of any offence in respect of parents and significant carers of youths aged 10 - 15, if it is considered desirable in the interests of preventing further offending or anti-social behaviour. Reasons must be given if an order is not made in respect of this age group, e.g. parenting is being addressed voluntarily or through another court order. The order becomes discretionary if the youth is aged 16 - 17. An order may also be made on the specific application of the youth offending team (yot).

The order involves two aspects:
- To comply with specific requirements for up to 12 months, and
- To attend for a period not exceeding 3 months, a counselling and guidance programme as may be specified by the responsible officer (usually a yot officer).

A report from the yot should be obtained so that the family circumstances are available to the court before making the order. Application may be made to vary or discharge the order.

- ❏ Breach = level 3 fine (£1,000)
- 🕐 Requirements up to 12 months
- 🕐 Sessions up to 3 months.

Future references to parent will assume parent and guardian.

10.3.4. Responsibility for money orders. See 10.6.3.

10.3.5. Views on proposed sentence. See 10.4.4.

10.4. Procedure in youth court

10.4.1. Informality

The proceedings in youth court are conducted informally in order to encourage youth and parent to take an active part and provide the fullest picture possible. This enables the court to select the most suitable penalty to address both welfare issues and the prevention of further offending. The risk of further offending is obviously a key indicator and material information is more likely to emerge in the youth courtroom than in the adult courtroom.

The chairman ensures that a communicative atmosphere is created from the outset, by identifying everyone who is in the courtroom, by frequent use of the youth's first name, and an encouragement for everyone to be seated. This applies particularly to the parent who is not on trial and who is likely to hold the greatest amount of useful information to assist the court.

10.4.2. Engagement with youth and parent

The youth is normally asked to give his name, address and date of birth, and who has come along with him, so that he is speaking from an early stage, rather than just nodding a response. Following the plea and prosecution outline/application, the defence solicitor will normally address the court before the court invites comment or asks specific questions of youth and parent.

When a youth is found guilty of an offence or in proceedings involving community orders, both the youth and parent must be given the opportunity of making a statement. The court must take into consideration all available information about general conduct, home surroundings, school record and medical history.

As with adult court, there is more likely to be a helpful response if it is understood that the reason for asking is to gather information so that the most appropriate and useful sentence is given, rather than to make matters worse. It may well build on what the defence solicitor has had to say. The main issue is to try and identify the underlying cause(s) to be addressed, so that the level and type of risk can be addressed.

Examples:

To the youth

1. 'We want to stop you getting into any more trouble by choosing the best way of doing that. Your solicitor says that too much alcohol/being easily led by your friends .... is the problem. Tell us about that.
2. What did you do on your Action Plan Order? What did you like best?

To the parent

3. 'Did you know that your son was in the city centre at 4 a.m.?'
4. 'When did he last go to school?'
5. 'What is his behaviour like at home?'

10.4.3. Reports

A report by the yot may be necessary to obtain sufficient information to sentence, and will be required to address suitability for most options. As with adult court, this may be achieved either by stand down from court or by a full pre-sentence report. The stand down is available for the most straightforward of penalties - courts vary in their guidance on this. Any report must normally be made available to the parent and the youth. The exceptions are if it is considered to be impracticable due to his age/understanding or the potential for serious harm, if he reads the full content and a verbal summary would be sufficient unless impracticable.

10.4.4. Views on proposed sentence

It is a statutory requirement that, before disposing of the case the court must tell the youth and parent of the manner in which it proposes to deal with the case and allow any representations to be made, unless it is considered undesirable to inform the youth as well. It may well be that parent has been present during a stand down enquiry and it is simply a question of checking his understanding of what has been discussed, and ensuring that there is no further comment about the proposal. When the order is made the court must explain the nature and effect of the order.

The relationship between parent and child is likely to be particularly strained, sensitive and tenuous as a result of the court proceedings. Every effort must be made to ensure that the relationship is on an even keel after the hearing by avoiding over-intrusive or patronising lines of enquiry. It is a positive sign that the parent has attended voluntarily. The ideal is that they feel that their input has been valued, their child has been respected and they believe that the court decision will help to stop further offending.

10.4.5. Grave crimes

The youth court cannot impose custody at all upon youths under the age of 12. Between the ages of 12 and 14 the power is limited to persistent offenders only. In the case of 15 to 17 year olds the maximum period of detention is 2 years (see 10.7.). Note that this is longer than the 6 months maximum custody which is currently available in the adult court, More serious crimes are therefore sentenced in the youth court than in the adult court. The top range of offences and offenders must be committed to the Crown Court. This is so that custodial powers may be used in respect of the younger age group, and for detention beyond 2 years for the persistent offenders and older age group. Specific provisions for committal apply to homicide and some firearm offences. The 'grave crimes' procedure applies to the remainder of the most serious crimes.

'Grave crimes' are offences which would be punishable in the adult court with 14 years or more, e.g. burglary, robbery, handling stolen goods, wounding with intent. They also include some specifically listed offences which do not carry 14 years, e.g. some sexual offences. When such offences are before the court, the initial decision is whether or not the matter should be committed to the Crown Court as a 'grave crime'.

The first decision for such cases is venue, rather than plea. Representations are made by prosecution and defence as to whether such offences should be dealt with by the youth court or be committed to the Crown Court. Previous convictions may be referred to. The prosecution facts should be taken at their highest at this stage, e.g. that he did use a knife. The defence will normally give an informal indication of plea.

Helpful guidance on this aspect of the decision-making process was given in R (on the application of H, A and O' v. Southampton Youth Court (2004) as follows:

Those under 15 should be tried in the youth court wherever possible. It is better designed for youths than the Crown Court 'with the inevitably greater formality and greatly increased number of people involved (including a jury and the public) and should be reserved for the most serious cases'. Further, that 'generally speaking, first-time offenders aged 12 to 14 and all offenders under 12 should not be detained in custody and decisions as to jurisdiction should have regard to the fact. In each case the court should ask itself whether there is a real prospect, having regard to his or her age, that this defendant might require a sentence of, or in excess of 2 years'. In respect of those who do not qualify for custody in the youth court, 'whether there is some unusual feature' requiring committal for custody. The fact that a youth does not qualify for a custodial sentence in the youth court is not regarded as an exceptional circumstance to justify committal.

10.4.6. Dangerous offenders

Bearing in mind the limitation on powers in the youth court, there are also provisions for sending for trial or committing for sentence those offenders who are deemed to be dangerous to the Crown Court. They may be sentenced as a 'dangerous offender' for longer periods than the statutory maximum custodial periods, e.g. a life sentence is available for robbery which normally carries 14 years.

The determination can only be made in respect of specified violent and sexual offences. Most of them are also 'grave crimes', but some of them are not because they do not carry 14 years, e.g. assault occasioning actual bodily harm. The test in respect of the specified offences is, whether there is a significant risk to members of the public of serious harm by this offender committing further specified offences. The court must consider the nature and circumstance of the offence which will normally be fully available from prosecution and defence. It may also consider any information about the pattern of behaviour and any information about the offender which is only likely to be explored fully at the report stage.

In clear cases, a determination can be made on the basis of the facts of the offence and the nature of the record. The youth will either be dealt with in the youth court immediately or sent directly to the Crown Court as a 'dangerous offender'. In other cases it should be stated that the determination as to whether the youth is deemed to be dangerous or not will be deferred until the conclusion of the case when full information is available. This does not prevent the case proceeding as a committal to Crown Court on the basis of it being a 'grave crime'. The facts of the offence clearly require more than a 2 year DTO, but the record does not create any major concern and there is not a report to assess whether there is a 'significant risk of serious harm' in future by this offender. This would leave the Judge to determine dangerousness at the report stage, if convicted, just as the magistrates would if the case were tried in the youth court.

In summary:
- Committal to Crown Court as a 'grave crime' - maximum penalty available at Crown Court includes custody for all youths up to the statutory maximum. Note that this determination must be made as an initial decision but the 'dangerous' determination may be deferred until after trial and report.

- Sending for trial or committing for sentence to Crown Court as a 'dangerous offender' - the maximum penalty available at Crown Court increases from the statutory maximum depending upon the type of offence, e.g. life for robbery.

10.4.7. Case management in youth court

The same principles of avoiding delay apply to the youth court just as in the adult court. Note that the Criminal Case Management Framework does not apply to youth court (see 6.1.). In the youth court the main difference is that some individuals are fast-tracked through the system, and in all cases, there is far greater liaison with other agencies to ensure that welfare and prevention of further offending are addressed from pre-court to the conclusion of any sentence. It is particularly in the interest of a youth that he is acquitted or sentenced quickly and rehabilitated quickly if necessary. Time is of the essence to divert from a criminal lifestyle before it becomes ingrained.

- **Persistent Young Offenders**

In 1996 the national average time from arrest through to sentence for youths was 142 days - 5 months. By 2002, one of the five government manifesto pledges was to reduce that period by a half to 71 days in respect of persistent young offenders. The term ' persistent young offender' (PYO) is basically a youth who is aged between 10 and 17 who has been sentenced on 3 or more separate occasions and the last one is within the last 3 years.

Whilst there is urgency to acquit or sentence effectively in all youth cases, the resource spotlight is upon PYOs. All agencies, including the court, prioritise actions e.g. preparation of committal papers, reports, and listing of trials so that they are expedited through the system.
The current targets for PYOs are:

- Charge to first appearance = 7 days for venue/plea
- Mode of trial to committal = 3 weeks for committal
- Conviction to sentence = 14 days for reports
- Not guilty plea to trial = 28 days for trial.

By May 2005 the national average period from arrest to sentence had fallen for PYOs from 142 days to 65 days.

- **Prolific and Priority Offenders (PPOs)**

This is another priority group based on the fact that around 10% of offenders are responsible for around 50% of all crime. They are identified by the police and other agencies based upon the nature and volume of their criminality and the nature and volume of the harm they are causing. Many PYOs will also be PPOs. There are three strands to this policy - to prevent and deter, to catch and convict, and then to rehabilitate and resettle. In order to ensure this happens, all agencies provide a premium service, particularly for the youths who are in this group of offenders.

10.5. Remand provisions

The table below summarises the options available, which are bail, remand to local authority accommodation, secure accommodation or prison/remand centre, for males and females in each age group.

Age	Gender	Remand - What is available?
All: 10 - 17	Male and female	Unconditional or conditional bail
All: 10 - 16	Male and female	Local Authority Accommodation with or without conditions
12 - 16 only	Female	Secure Accommodation
12 - 14 only	Male	Secure Accommodation
15 - 16 only	Male	Secure Accommodation only if deemed to be vulnerable, otherwise Prison/ Remand Centre
17 only	Male and female	Prison/Remand Centre

10.5.5. Bail - unconditional and conditional

The Bail Act provisions apply as for adults and the starting point is unconditional bail (see chapter 8). However, there are a few practical and legal differences if conditions are justified:

- The 'live and sleep' bail condition is often defined as 'where directed by the local authority/youth offending team' to allow scope for effective placement and movement if necessary - often away from parent initially and then perhaps with a staged return.
- The curfew condition may include the additional proviso, 'unless accompanied' by a named person. This may be the parent so that the parent is not restricted indoors as well. It may be a youth offending team (yot) officer, so that supervised activities can take place. This would not be practical if an electronic curfew is attached.
- Electronic curfews (tagging) are available for youths aged 12 - 16 (age 17 in some areas), but they are limited to serious charges e.g. robbery, and to youths who repeatedly commit offences whilst on bail or in local authority accommodation.
- A condition may be attached where appropriate for the youth to comply with bail supervision and support. The yot must be consulted to determine suitable support activities, and failure to comply with the instructions of the supervising officer is a breach of bail.
- Where available, the more serious bail risk may be made subject to the more stringent condition to comply with the Intensive Supervision and Surveillance Programme (ISSP) as a bail condition. There are two alternative scenarios for ISSP. The first scenario arises if it is at least the 5th separate occasion that the youth is facing a charge in the last 12 months and he has received at least one community or custodial penalty - the prolific offender in a short space of time. The second scenario is if he satisfies the criteria for a remand to secure accommodation (see below). Compliance with the ISSP condition includes at least 25 hours per week of contact from the youth offending team and at least 2 surveillance contacts per day.
- The condition 'not to associate with the co-accused' arises more often than in the adult court - peer pressure is a key factor in youth crime.
- A parental surety of up to £50 may be ordered with the parent's consent to ensure compliance with conditions - rare, but possible.

10.5.6. Bail refused

- **Remand to prison/remand centre**

So far as refusal of bail is concerned, a youth of 17 is remanded to prison custody or a remand centre, just as an 18 year old in the adult court.

- **Remand to local authority accommodation**

For the age 10 to 16 group, the most common option is to remand to local authority accommodation. This may be in a children's home, foster home, specialist remand foster carer, or even a return to family if this is considered to be appropriate.

It is important to recognise that the remand 'to local authority accommodation' does not confer any parental responsibility on the local authority. After consultation with the local authority, the court may add any conditions except a condition as to residence, as this would effectively take away the discretion to place the youth as considered appropriate by the local authority. The power to move the youth from place to place as circumstance changes is important in the process of preventing offending and rehabilitating, and must not be fettered. The court may however, specify that the child/young person is not placed with a named individual e.g. co-accused adult. It may also impose requirements on the authority to make sure that the remand conditions are complied with

Breach of the conditions may result in arrest and reconsideration of bail. At any time, whilst on remand to local authority accommodation, the authority may request that they place the youth into secure accommodation if criteria are satisfied e.g. that there is a history of absconding and he has been charged with a further offence during the remand period.

- **Remand to secure accommodation**

Remands to secure accommodation apply to youths of 12 upwards. The first remand may well be straight to secure accommodation. The criteria is complicated but can be summarised basically as two key scenarios:

- That they have been convicted or charged with a serious offence, and they present a risk of serious harm to the public which cannot be met in any other way
or
- They have a history of offending on bail or in local authority accommodation, and that it is the only way to prevent further offending.

The youth offending team (yot) must be consulted to consider alternatives e.g. bail supervision and support, ISSP, electronic curfew as a condition of bail.

The accommodation is a secure children's home for girls aged 12 to 16, and for boys aged 12 to 14.

- **Remand to remand centre/prison for boys of 15/16**

When the secure accommodation criteria are met, boys of 15 and 16 are sent to a remand centre or prison, unless they are deemed to be 'vulnerable', physically or emotionally, and then they may be placed in a secure children's home instead. The information as to vulnerability is provided to the court by the yot.

10.6. Sentencing options in youth court

10.6.1. Referral Order

This applies to all youths who do not have a previous conviction or bind over, and they have pleaded guilty to an imprisonable offence. The only alternative sentences are at the extremes of absolute discharge or custody (or a hospital order if appropriate). Where the offence is not imprisonable, the referral order is discretionary and it is a matter for the court whether they choose a referral order or not.

The referral order has the specific aim of preventing further offending and the hope is that it will be the first and last order for the individual. A local Youth Offending Panel, which includes a yot officer and two members of the local community agree a contract with the youth and parent. The parent must be ordered to attend the initial meeting and progress meetings of the Panel (youth aged 10-16) unless it would be unreasonable, and they may be ordered to attend if the youth is 17.

The contract includes some community payback; intervention to address risk factors, e.g. constructive leisure programme, and a guidance/monitoring element with contact at least every fortnight with the yot officer for the first half of the order. The terms may include specific provisions, e.g. to keep away from specified places or persons, school attendance etc. and they will be reviewed by the panel. A parenting order may now be considered in addition but a yot report is required to address the need for making both orders. Compensation, disqualification/endorsement and costs may be ordered in addition.

Where the order is not complied with, the panel may review, and/or vary the terms by consent, or refer the case back to court. A referral back to court is accompanied by a report explaining why it has been necessary to refer back to court - the facts and how any discretion has been exercised. If is proved that the panel acted reasonably, and the panel decision is upheld, the court may revoke the referral order and may re-sentence the youth in any way that it could have been sentenced originally. This must take into account the extent of compliance with the order.

When a further offence is committed before the referral order, the court may extend the period of the order. If a further offence is committed after the referral order begins, then it may also extend the period but must find exceptional circumstances to justify this. The ultimate sanction is to revoke the order and re-sentence.

The latest Home Office reconviction data show that 60% of youths who were made subject to a referral order have not re-offended during a 2 year period since their orders commenced. Longer term data is not available as the referral order was only rolled out nationally, just over 2 years ago.

- ❏ Breach: Revoke and re-sentence for breach of requirements
  Extend order up to 12 months maximum in respect of further offence
- ⏱ Minimum of 3 months to 12 months from the date of signing the contract.

10.6.2. Absolute or Conditional Discharge

The provisions are the same as for an adult with two limitations. Where a youth has received a Final Warning, and is convicted of an offence within 2 years of the Warning, the court must not impose a conditional discharge unless there are exceptional circumstances relating to the offence or the offender. A conditional discharge cannot be imposed instead of a Referral Order - only an absolute discharge.

Conditional discharges were previously the most common penalties in youth court, but they have now been taken over by the Referral Order as the usual first option for most youths.

10.6.3. Fine, Compensation and Costs

- **Maxima**

The maximum fine is less than for an adult:

Youth aged 10 -13 = Maximum of £250
Youth aged 14 -17 = Maximum of £1000.

A proportionate reduction of fine is anticipated in proportion to the adult maximum of £5000. This may be reflected by ensuring that the fine is payable within 3 months rather than the maximum of the 12 month period for an adult. This argument is also supported by the fact that most orders made in the youth court for low seriousness do not extend beyond 3 months.

The maximum compensation order is the same as in the adult court - £5,000 per offence.

If the youth is ordered to pay the fine, then the amount of costs cannot exceed the amount of the fine. If the fine is £5 or less, there can be no order for costs.

- **Who pays?**

The parent/guardian of a 10 - 15 year old <u>must</u> pay, on the basis of their means, unless they cannot be found, or it would be unreasonable to so order, e.g. the youth is in local authority care and has no contact with either parent.

The parent/guardian of a 16 - 17 year old may be ordered to pay, e.g. the youth is in employment. If this is simply a part-time job, the fine may be very low, e.g. £12 per week for a paper round, with credit for a guilty plea would be a £9 fine. Note that costs would be limited to £9. The parent may well pay and hope for reimbursement. If a local authority has parental responsibility then an order may be made against the local authority unless it would be unreasonable to do so, e.g. the authority has done all it reasonably could to protect the public from the offender. Representations must always be invited before the order is made.

- **Default**

So far as default is concerned, if the youth is ordered to pay, there is no power to order detention in default, but there are two additional options. They are, an order requiring his parent to enter a recognisance to ensure the fine is paid by consent (very rare) or an order for the parent to pay if the youth has refused or neglected to pay but has had the means to do so. Full enforcement provisions apply to a parent who is ordered to pay, including custody.

10.6.4. Reparation Order

This is available for all youths and falls below the level of a community order. It may be used for non-imprisonable first offences if a Referral Order is not considered to be appropriate, or for subsequent minor offences. The youth is placed under the supervision of a responsible officer. Reparation is either to a specified person with their consent (direct), or to the community at large but bearing some relationship to the crime (indirect). The order is based very much on the principle of restorative justice and if a face to face meeting can be organised with the victim, this will be the main thrust of the order. The reality is that many victims do not want to engage to this extent, but some are prepared to receive a letter of apology. A report must be obtained to indicate the type of action or work which is suitable for the youth and whether the victim is prepared to engage if known. It may not be combined with a community order or custody.

- ❑ Breach - no action; fine up to £1,000; attendance centre order; curfew order; revoke the order and re-sentence.
- ☻ All age groups
- ☻ No minimum. Up to 24 hours over a period of up to 3 months.

SERIOUS ENOUGH
Community orders for youths

A report is required in all cases and all orders may subsequently be varied and breached. The Sentencing Guidelines Council state that 'a reduction for sentence should be applied to any punitive elements' e.g. curfew order, attendance centre order. In the youth court, most penalties are based upon rehabilitation rather than punishment, and additionally some are for fixed periods and it is not therefore possible to express credit in many cases.

10.6.5. Action Plan Order

The plan consists of a series of requirements in respect of actions and whereabouts during the order, under the supervision of a responsible officer who gives directions. The requirements may include various aspects:

- Participation in activities at time/place specified
- Present himself to specified persons at time/place specified
- Attend the attendance centre (imprisonable offences only)
- Stay away from specified places
- Comply with education requirements
- Make reparation
- Attend a progress hearing in court within 21 days of making the order.

- ❏ Breach - no action; fine up to £1,000; attendance centre order; curfew order; revoke and re-sentence.
- ⏱ All age groups
- ⏱ 3 months fixed period (cannot therefore be reduced by a guilty plea).

10.6.6. Attendance Centre

The offence must be imprisonable. The centre must be accessible for the particular youth. A youth aged up to 14 may be expected to travel up to 10 miles or for 45 minutes (one way), and aged 14 or over up to 15 miles or for 90 minutes. The longer the journey, the greater the restriction on liberty and this may be reflected in the hours ordered. The court must specify the first attendance and the officer in charge fixes the future sessions. Sessions cover practical activities, group work and discussion. There may be difficulties with youths who have problems integrating with others, e.g. those who are excluded from school for this reason, and those who really need one to one advice to deal with underlying welfare problems. It is important to check with the yot as to suitability.

- ❏ Breach - No action: fine up to £1,000; revoke and re-sentence.
- ⏱ Age 10 -13: Less than 12 hours if this is considered excessive due to age and circumstances
- ⏱ Age 10 - 15: 12 to 24 hours
- ⏱ Age 16 - 17: 12 to 36 hours
- ⏱ Up to 3 hours per session.

10.6.7. Supervision Order

The supervisor is under a duty to advise, assist and befriend, and contact begins at the rate of twice weekly for the first 3 months and then decreases. The order does not automatically carry any standard requirements, but the court will normally impose standard requirements in all orders to keep in touch with the supervising officer, notify any change of address and receive home visits. Other requirements are specific to the individual and may include the following:

- ❑ To reside with a named individual with their consent, e.g. live with mother
- ❑ To comply with the directions of the supervisor for up to 180 days i.e. 6 months (specified activities by the supervisor - not specified by the court)
- ❑ To live at a specified place; present himself to specified person/place/time; take part in activities at a specified place/time; make reparation - for up to 180 days (intermediate treatment - specified by the court)
- ❑ To refrain from specified activities on specified days or for the whole of the order
- ❑ To comply with arrangements for education - not necessarily to 'go to school'

Specific qualifying criteria apply to the following:
- Live in local authority accommodation up to 6 months
- Live with local authority foster parent up to 12 months
- Treatment for mental health condition
- Drug treatment and testing (pilot areas only).

It was previously possible to impose a night restriction requirement. This has been repealed and has been overtaken by the curfew order.

- Intensive Supervision and Surveillance Programme (ISSP) - pilot areas only

The programme may be included as a specific requirement within a supervision order. It is designed for the most serious offenders who are otherwise at risk of custody. This is reflected in the minimum period of 25 hours per week with the youth offending team. The programme addresses the causes of offending behaviour e.g. substance misuse, peer influence, withdrawal from education. The surveillance aspect ensures that the youth is being watched and checked in the community, by tracking, electronic tagging, and/or intelligence-led policing. The ISSP requirement is normally for the full 180 days / 6 months, but longer periods are currently being piloted.

- ❑ Breach - No action; fine up to £1,000; attendance centre order; curfew order; revoke and re-sentence.
- ⏰ All age groups
- ⏰ No minimum. Up to 3 years.

10.6.8. Curfew Order

The order is accompanied by electronic tagging, and may involve different addresses and different times each day if appropriate. The daily period is from 2 hours to 12 hours. The likely impact on family circumstances must be checked out first. Keeping a reluctant teenager indoors could either push family life over the edge or could be a valuable aid to exerting some control. The custodian will usually be the parent or care officer and their views are very helpful. See 8.17.

- ❏ Breach - No order; attendance centre order; curfew order; community punishment order up to 60 hours if aged16+; revocation and re-sentence.
- ⏲ Age 10 - 15: Up to 3 months (pilot areas = 6 months)
- ⏲ Age 16 - 17: Up to 6 months.

10.6.9. Adult community orders for 16 and 17 year olds

See 8.13 for full details. The orders below remain in existence in the youth court, but are restricted to offences committed prior to April 2005 for adults. The generic community order has taken over from the individual orders in the adult court, but not in the youth court. Unlike the community order, the orders cannot be re-opened and re-sentenced on commission of a further offence.

- Community Rehabilitation Order
- Community Punishment Order
- Combination Order
- Drug Treatment and Testing Order.

10.7. Detention and Training Order (DTO)

The Detention and Training Order is a two part sentence which includes a period of custody (detention) and a period of supervision in the community. It is for a fixed period of 4,6,8,10,12,18 or 24 months.

Criteria:

- Either, the offence must be so serious that only a custodial sentence is justified, or
  It is a violent or sexual offence and the court is satisfied that only such a sentence is adequate to protect the public from serious harm.
- Youths of 10 and 11 cannot be given a Detention and Training Order DTO).
- Youths aged between 12 and 14 may be given a DTO if they are 'persistent offenders'.

'Persistent offender' is defined broadly and is not connected at all with the 'persistent young offender' (PYO) initiative. It is simply to avoid first time offenders being give a DTO in the 12 to 14 age group, unless there is a series of offences before the court, when he may properly be regarded as a 'persistent offender'. He has not been caught and convicted for each offence as they happened, but they all fall to be dealt with together as the same 'big picture' of persistent offending.

Unlike the adult court, the court must take account of the remand period in custody at the point of determining the length of sentence. It is not simply a case of announcing that the number of days served are to be taken into account. They must be calculated into the actual sentence. For example, if a youth has served 8 weeks on remand in custody, this is the equivalent of a 16 week (4 month) sentence, and he could be given a 4 month order instead of a 8 month order on this basis. There is no remission on a DTO - half is served in custody and the other half is served in the community with restriction on liberty throughout the period.

The Secretary of State determines any early release, e.g. on compassionate grounds; by a period of no more than 2 months. He may also apply to the court for late release of up to 2 months depending upon the length of the order. This is rare.

A supervising officer is appointed at the start of the sentence and an initial training plan is drawn up within 5 days of admission to address offending behaviour and development needs. For example this may include completing a number of hours of literacy and numeracy, completing group work programmes without misbehaviour, and applying for, and then attending a training course upon release. Upon release, a supervision notice is served, and the supervising officer makes a home visit within 5 days and then he has contact twice weekly during the first 3 months, and then reducing. Many youths undertake the Intensive Supervision and Surveillance Programme (see 10.6.7.) as the main element of the community part of the sentence - breach may result in a fine or a return to detention.

If the youth is convicted of a further imprisonable offence during the order, the court may order an additional period of detention. The maximum period is the length of time between the date of the new offence and the original DTO expiry date. Basically, he is liable to serve in detention from the day of the new offence (if convicted) to the end of the order. This is a powerful deterrent against further offending during the supervision period. It may be served concurrently or consecutively to the sentence for the new offence.

It is clear in case law that credit must be given for a guilty plea in the calculation of a DTO period, Obviously the periods fixed do not always lend themselves to a strict 1/3. For example, a DTO for 2 years was reduced to 18 months in order to reflect the guilty plea.

- ❏ Breach of requirement during supervision: Fine up to £1,000, or detention for remainder of order or 3 months, whichever is the less
- ✪ Fixed periods of 4,6,8,10,12,18 or 24 months, but the court may make consecutive sentences which do not add up to these figures, e.g. 8 months + 6 months = 14 months.

Sentence may be deferred on youths (although this is rare), and ancillary orders are equally available in the youth court e.g. bolt-on ASBO, disqualification. See 8.34 to 8.46.

10.8. Structured sentencing for youths

10.8.1. 4 'O' structure

The principle of the 4 'O' structure applies in the same way as for adults with the modifications as below.

Offence

Consult the Youth Court Bench Book Guidelines at part 2. The Guidelines give an entry point of seriousness for each offence based on 'low', 'medium' and 'high' which further defines the Adult Sentencing Guidelines for youth sentencing purposes. For example, the Adult Guidelines give theft as a community entry point. The Youth Guidelines break this down further and theft from a shop is given as 'low' with theft from a person as 'high'.

Offender

The most important feature is the assessment of the individual's risk of re-offending so that an appropriate penalty can be imposed, often with an entirely individual package of support,

Some typical questions for assessing risk level are listed below:

- What is the pattern (if any) of any previous convictions?
- What response (if any) has been made to previous sentences?
- Is there a supportive family? Does parent attend court?
- In what type of accommodation are they living?
- Is education being pursued?
- What is their employment status?
- Is there evidence of responding to peer pressure?
- Excess alcohol?
- Illegal drug use? How is this being managed?
- What is their attitude towards offending?
- Is there motivation to change?

Much of this information is identified by the youth offending team, building upon their ongoing information record for youths who appear before the court. This is known as an ASSET record. It includes care history, criminal history, education, health, analysis of offending, indicators of harm to others and indicators of vulnerability. The information for youth court is therefore, more detailed with persistent offenders than in the adult court.

Objective(s)

Always the same - To have regard to the welfare of the youth and prevent further offending

Options

The most appropriate option within the seriousness band.

10.8.2. The Sentencing Matrix

The Sentencing Guidelines Council is currently preparing sentencing guidelines specifically for youths. In the meantime, the current guidance is set out in the Youth Bench Book on the offence by offence basis above, which then links into the sentencing matrix below.

	LOW RISK of re-offending	MEDIUM RISK of re-offending	HIGH RISK of re-offending
LOW LEVEL Seriousness	Conditional discharge Fine Compensation Reparation Order	Conditional Discharge Fine Compensation Reparation Order	Fine Compensation Reparation Order
MEDIUM LEVEL Seriousness	Reparation Order Attendance Centre Order Action Plan Order	Attendance Centre Order Action Plan Order Supervision Order *CRO *CPO	Action Plan Order Supervision Order CRO + requirements CPO Curfew Order
HIGH LEVEL Seriousness	Action Plan Order Supervision Order *CRO *CPO Combination Order Detention and Training Order	Action Plan Order Supervision Order *CRO *CPO Combination Order Curfew Detention and Training Order	Supervision Order CRO + requirements Combination Order Drug Treatment and Testing Order Detention and Training Order

*CRO = Community Rehabilitation Order
*CPO = Community Punishment Order

10.8.3 Sentencing examples

Taking an example of shoplifting, and using the structured approach along with the sentencing matrix above.

Offence entry point = Low

Aggravating features = High value. Planned expedition. Organised team. Sophisticated methods. Additional offences to be taken into consideration.
Mitigating features = None.
Offence seriousness increases from Low to High.

Offender information = Age 16.
Previous convictions for theft and burglary.
Failure to comply with current Action Plan Order.
Parent attends court on warrant.
Living with drug-using friends.
Heroin user.
Unemployed.
Risk of re-offending is High.

Objective
Regard to welfare needs e.g. accommodation, drug use and the need to prevent escalation of offending any further.

Options? (High/high)
Drug Treatment and Testing Order <u>or</u>
Supervision Order with condition to comply with full 180 days of directions (possibly Intensive Supervision and Surveillance Programme), <u>or</u> Drug Treatment and Testing condition (if available locally).

This scenario can be compared with the situation of a youth who steals a single item on impulse, and only has a single theft conviction for which he was given a 3 month referral order which he has completed. He is attending school, and parent accompanies to court. A Reparation Order with compensation would be the most likely sentencing option (Low/low).

The youth court has a wide range of excellent options available to it. It is essential to use every possible source of information to the full - the prosecutor, the defence solicitor, the youth offending team, and the people who really know the situation better than anyone else, the parent and the young person. The optimism of youth court work is the fact that many defendants do not come back to court again, and some of the regular youth court attenders never see the inside of an adult court. Youth justice is working!

COMMON ABBREVIATIONS

I have tried to avoid using abbreviations except when they follow the full description, but it is worth being 'up to date' with the inevitable 'court-speak'. If in doubt - ask.

ABC	Acceptable Behaviour Contract (not a court order)
ABO	Attachment of Benefit Order (money order collection)
AEO	Attachment of Earnings Order
AI or AD	Advance Information/Disclosure from the prosecution to defence
ASBO	Anti Social Behaviour Order
ASRO	Addressing Substance Related Offending accredited programme
BR	Bail Refused
BTDC	Bench Training and Development Committee
CD	Conditional Discharge
CJA	Criminal Justice Act 2003
CJIT	Criminal Justice Integrated Teams (drug user through care)
CMF	Case Management Framework (emphasis on avoiding delays)
CRASBO	Criminal Anti Social Behaviour Order - 'bolt-on' to sentence
DIDs	Drink Impaired Drivers accredited programme
DJ (MC)	District Judge (Magistrates' Court)
DIP	Drug Intervention Programme (voluntary and bail)
DDRS	Drink Drive Rehabilitation Scheme (reduced disqualification)
DTTO	Drug Treatment and Testing Order
DVLA	Driver & Vehicle Licensing Authority
ETJ	Elects Trial by Jury (either-way offences)
ETS	Enhanced Thinking Skills accredited programme
FDR	Fast Delivery Report (usually on stand down from court)
GOP	General Offending accredited Programme, includes ETS
IC	In Custody (on remand)
IDAP	Integrated Domestic Abuse accredited Programme
ISO	Individual Support Order (youths on ASBOs)
ISSP	Intensive Supervision and Surveillance Programme
MATC	Magistrates Area Training Committee
MNTI	Magistrates National Training Initiative
MOT	Mode of Trial (Magistrates' or Crown Court?)
NAB	No Application for Bail
NOMS	National Offender Management Service
OPL	Driver 'Over the Prescribed Limit' (alcohol)
PBV	Plea Before Venue
PPO	Persistent and Prolific Offender (youths and adults - premium service)
PSR	Pre-sentence Report

PTR	Pre-Trial Review
PYO	Persistent Young Offender
ROB	Restriction on Bail (if positive drug test given)
SDR	Standard Delivery Report (3-4 weeks)
SSR	Specific Sentence Report (usually on stand down from court)
SOPO	Sex Offender Protection Order
STNA	Summary Trial Not Appropriate (either-way offences)
TICs	Offences Taken Into Consideration as schedule of admissions
TWOC	Take motor vehicle Without Owner's Consent
Yot	Youth offending team

USEFUL WEBSITES

Criminal Justice System Online
www.cjsonline.gov.uk

Crown Prosecution Service
www.cps.gov.uk

Department of Constitutional Affairs
www.dca.gov.uk

Home Office
www.homeoffice.gov.uk

HM Prison Service
www.hmprisonservice.gov.uk

Judicial Studies Board
www.jsboard.co.uk

Magistrates Association.
www.magistrates-association.org.uk

Magistrates' Court
www.courtservice.gov.uk

National Probation Service
www.probation.homeoffice.gov.uk

National Statistics Online - Census 2001
www.statistics.gov.uk/census2001

Victim Support
www.victimsupport.org.uk

Witness Service
www.victimsupport.org.uk/services/witness_services.html

Youth Justice Board
www.youth-justice-board.gov.uk

BIBLIOGRAPHY

Carr, A. P. and Turner, A. J. (eds.) (2005) *Stone's Justices' Manual 2005*. 137th ed. 3 vols. London: LexisNexis Butterworths.

Criminal Justice System (2005) *Criminal Case Management Framework*. 2nd ed. London: CJS.

Judicial Studies Board (2001) *Equality before the Courts: a Short Practical Guide for Judges*. London: Judicial Studies Board.

Judicial Studies Board (2005) *Youth Court Bench Book*. London: Judicial Studies Board.

Judicial Studies Board (2005) *Adult Court Bench Book*. London: Judicial Studies Board.

Judicial Studies Board (2003) *Magistrates National Training Initiative Handbook: MNTI 2*. London: Judicial Studies Board.

Justices' Clerks' Society (2000) *Fair Treatment Pack*. London: Justices' Clerks' Society. Winchester: Waterside Press.

Keogh, A. (ed.) (2005) *Criminal Procedure Rules 2005: Case Management Resources*. London: The Law Society.

Mimmack, A. (2005) *"Deferred sentences - a familiar power with new teeth"*. In: *The Magistrate,* vol.61, no.7, p.219.

Moore, T. G. (ed.) (2004) *Anthony & Berryman's Magistrates' Courts Guide 2005*. London: LexisNexis Butterworths.

National Probation Service (2005) *Probation Circular Reference no. PC57/2005: Effective Management of the Drug Rehabilitation Requirement (DRR) and Alcohol Treatment Requirement (ATR)*. London: National Probation Directorate.

National Probation Service (2005) *National Standards 2005 (Minimum National Standards for Service Delivery)*. London: Secretary of State for the Home Department.

Sentencing Guidelines Council (2004) *New Sentences: Criminal Justice Act 2003: Guideline*. London: Sentencing Guidelines Secretariat.

Sentencing Guidelines Council (2004) *Overarching Principles: Seriousness: Guideline.* London: Sentencing Guidelines Secretariat.

Sentencing Guidelines Council (2004) *Reduction in Sentence for a Guilty Plea: Guideline.* London: Sentencing Guidelines Secretariat.

Ward, R. and Davies, O.M. (2004) *The Criminal Justice Act 2003: A Practitioner's Guide.* Bristol: Jordans.

APPENDIX 1

Adult Court - Sentencing options menu

\	Increase of seriousness and restriction of liberty →			
Inexpedient to punish		'Serious enough'	'So serious'	Too Serious
			Custody	Commit to Crown Court
			Suspended sentence	
			Intermittent custody	
		Community Order Low Medium High	Community Order High	
	Compensation			
	Fine	Fine	Fine	
Conditional Discharge				
Absolute Discharge				

++ ANCILLARY PENALTIES - always seek representations first - check proportionate (see overleaf).

ANCILLARY PENALTIES

Penalty	Key points
Anti-Social Behaviour Order	Caused or likely to cause harassment, alarm or distress and order is necessary. 'Must not' requirements. Minimum of 2 years.
Binding Over Order	Future breach of peace apprehended. Amount and period to reflect seriousness of behaviour feared.
Compensation	Damage, injury, loss, or terror and distress.
Exclusion from licensed premises	Violence or threats of violence in licensed premises. 3 months to 2 years.
Re-test	Endorseable offence and 'concern for safety of other road users'. 'L' plates and passenger, or driver is committing offence of driving whilst disqualified instead of just the licence offences.
Disqualification	Also as a stand-alone penalty for all offences since January 2004.
Endorsement	Penalty points allocated to most serious on the occasion, or reasons given for separate points. 12 points = disqualification.
Football banning order	Relevant offences only + believe order will help prevent violence/disorder at designated matches. Minimum 3 years.
Restraining order	Only to offences under Protection from Harassment Act 1997 offences. Specific requirements. 'Until further order' maximum.
Sexual offences prevention order	Necessary to protect public or members of public from serious sexual harm.
Sex offender notification requirement	Relevant offences only - report details to police within 3 days. Period depends on sentence.
Parenting order	Child is convicted, ASBO, Sex Offender Order. Non-school attendance cases. Up to 12 months with counselling/guidance sessions.
Costs	Proportionate but not necessarily less than any fine imposed.
Forfeiture of property	Statutory powers e.g. drugs, offensive weapon.

APPENDIX 2 - FINES CALCULATOR

ANNUAL SALARY	2080	2340	2600	2860	3120	3380	3640	3900	4160	4420	4680	4940	5200	5460	5720	5980
MONTHLY	173	195	217	238	260	282	303	325	347	368	390	412	433	455	477	498
WEEKLY	40	45	50	55	60	65	70	75	80	85	90	95	100	105	110	115
BAND A	20	23	25	28	30	33	35	38	40	43	45	48	50	53	55	58
A(with credit)	13	15	17	18	20	22	23	25	27	28	30	32	33	35	37	38
BAND B	40	45	50	55	60	65	70	75	80	85	90	95	100	105	110	115
B(with credit)	27	30	33	37	40	43	47	50	53	57	60	63	67	70	73	77
BAND C	60	68	75	83	90	98	105	113	120	128	135	143	150	158	165	173
C(with credit)	40	45	50	55	60	65	70	75	80	85	90	95	100	105	110	115
ANNUAL SALARY	6240	6500	6760	7020	7280	7540	7800	8320	8840	9360	9880	10400	10920	11440	11960	12480
MONTHLY	520	542	563	585	607	628	650	693	737	780	823	867	910	963	997	1040
WEEKLY	120	125	130	135	140	145	150	160	170	180	190	200	210	220	230	240
BAND A	60	63	65	68	70	73	75	80	85	90	95	100	105	110	115	120
A(with credit)	40	42	43	45	47	48	50	53	57	60	63	67	70	73	77	80
BAND B	120	125	130	135	140	145	150	160	170	180	190	200	210	220	230	240
B(with credit)	80	83	87	90	93	97	100	107	113	120	127	133	140	147	153	160
BAND C	180	188	195	203	210	218	225	240	255	277	285	300	315	330	345	360
C(with credit)	120	125	130	135	140	145	150	160	170	180	190	200	210	220	230	240

Credit figure quoted as one third.
Acknowledgement to John Cook, J.P, Leeds.

INDEX

Abbreviations	176	Breach - community orders	107, 121
ABC approach	47	Burden of proof	63
Absolute discharge	94		
Accredited programmes	169	Case management	51
Addressing Substance Related		Case management duties	53
Offending	114	Case management questions	21
Adjournment of trial	59	Case management sanctions	56
Adjournments - questioning	21	Case progression form	54
Adjournments - reports	59	Case progression officers	51
Advance information	57	Charging order	102
Aggressive behaviour	12	Collection officers	103
Alcohol treatment	118	Collection orders	103
Ancillary orders	130	Combination order	106
Anti-social behaviour order	130	Committal for sentence	128
Appointment of a receiver	102	Committal for trial	71
Appraisal	10	Committal to prison - fines	102
Article 6	64	Community order	108
Article 8	68	Community order - breach	121
ASBO	130	Community order - further	
Assertive behaviour	12	offending	123
Attachment of benefits	100	Community penalty	106
Attachment of debts	101	Community punishment order	106
Attachment of earnings	100	Community rehabilitation order	104
Attendance centre - youths	169	Compensation	104
Attendance centre order - fines	102	Competence 1	1
Attendance centre	118	Competence 2	12
		Competence 3	17
		Competence 4	20
Bad character	81	Conditional discharge	94
Bail application	46	Conditions of bail	42
Bail conditions	42	Contempt of court	32
Bail procedure	46, 50	Contributions - effective	12
Bail refused	45	County Court	62
Bail - structured approach	47	Court hierarchy	61
Bail time limits	49	Court of Appeal	61
Bail TV link	50	Cracked trial	59
Bail	40	CRASBO	130
Behaviour - assertive	12	Credit for guilty plea	90
Bias	17	Criminal and Civil - differences	62
Bibliography	179	Criminal ASBO	130
Bind over	133	Criminal Case Management	
'Bolt-on' ASBO	130	Framework	51
Breach - suspended sentence	126	Criminal Procedure Rules	51

Cross-examination	73	Feedback	151
Crown Court	62	Final warning	157
Culpability	87	Fines	95
Culture	8	Fines - enforcement	99
Curfew Order - youths	170	Fines - youth	167
Curfew	112	Fines calculator	183
Custody	124	Fines payment work	103
		Fixed penalty ticket	157
Dangerous offenders	162	Football banning order	134
Deferred sentence	129	Foreign travel order	132
Delegated powers	146	Forfeiture order	136
Deprivation order	136		
Detention and Training Order	171	Garnishee proceedings	101
Development	9	General offending programme	113
Directions - standard	54	Grave crimes	161
Disability - dealing with	24	Guardianship order	118
Discharge - youth	167		
Discharge	94	Harm	87
Discourteous advocates	33	Hearsay evidence	80
Discretionary disqualification	139	Hierarchy of courts	61
Discriminatory comments	15	High Court	61
Disqualification	105, 138	High Court action - fines	101
Disqualification until test	141	High, medium, low range	109
Disruptive behaviour	31	Hospital order	117
Distress warrant	101	House of Lords	61
Doctrine of precedent	61	Human Rights Act 1998	64
Drink Impaired Drivers	114		
Drug Rehabilitation Requirement	114	Impartial tribunal	65
		Indictable only offences	68
Drug test on charge	40	Individual support order	131
Drug Treatment and Testing Order	107	Ineffective trial	59
		Integrated Domestic Abuse	114
		Intensive change and control	106
Effective trial management	59	Intensive Supervision and Surveillance	170
Either-way offences	69		
Electronic curfew	112	Interference with witnesses	45
Endorsement	137	Interim disqualification	141
Enforcement of fines	99	Intermittent custody	125
Engagement - youth court	159	ISSP	170
Enhanced Thinking Skills	113		
Equal treatment	23	Judicial oath	7
European Court Of Human Rights	61		
Evidence - basic rules	79	Language - non-discriminatory	14
Examination in chief	73	Learning styles	38
Exceptional hardship	29, 139	Learning	9
Exceptions to bail	41	Legal adviser - role	146
Exclusion order	133	Listening skills	3
Exclusion requirement	119	Local authority - remand	164
Failure to surrender to bail	48	Making judicial decisions	17
Fair treatment	8	Management Framework	51
Fast delivery report	110	Managing conflict	35

185

Managing decision-making	33	Questioning - mitigation	28
Managing disagreement	35	Questions - bench	5
Managing the proceedings	20	Questions - types of	21, 28
Managing yourself	1		
Mandatory disqualification	138	Race	8
Mental health treatment	119	Reasons - sentence	92
Mentored sittings	9	Reasons - verdict	76
Menu - sentencing options	181	Rectification	99
Mode of trial	69	Re-examination	74
Money Payment Supervision Order	01	Referral order	166
		Register of fines and judgements	103
		Relevant paperwork	1
Net income	96	Religion	8
Newton hearing	70	Remission	99
No case to answer	74	Reparation order	168
Non-verbal behaviour	3	Reports - adjournment	59
Not guilty - sequence	72	Reprimand	157
Note taking	3	Requirements - Community Order	111
		Residence requirement	118
Objectives of sentence	90	Responsible officer	110
Offence seriousness	87	Restraining order	135
Offender mitigation	89	Restriction on bail	40
One day detention - fines	100	Revocation of licence	142
One day detention	105	Right to a fair trial	64
Opening the court proceedings	22	Risk of sexual harm order	132
Order of proceedings	64	Role of the legal adviser	145
		Role of the winger	2
Parent/guardian - youths	158	Running commentary	23
Parental bind over	158		
Parenting Order	135	Sanctions - case management	56
Parenting order	158	Search warrants	77
Penalty points	137	Secure accommodation	165
Persistent Young Offenders	163	Security - bail	44
Points disqualification	139	Self development	38
Post-sitting review	10,149	Sentence reasons	92
Precedent	61	Sentencing - structure	86
Pre-court briefing	146	Sentencing matrix - youths	174
Pre-court interventions	157	Sentencing options menu	181
Prejudice	17	Serious enough	106
Press restrictions	65	Sex offender - registration	132
Previous convictions	89	Sex offenders programme	114
Priestley one to one	113	Sexual offences prevention order	132
Probation report	110	Special measures	24, 84
Prohibited activity	118	Special needs	23
Prolific and priority offenders	163	Special reasons	143
Pronouncements - content	25	Specified activity	118
Pronouncements - delivery	25	Speed camera offences	143
Publicity	65	Standard delivery report	110
Purposes of sentence	90	Standard of proof	63
		Stereotyping - challenge	15
Questioning - adjournments	21	Stereotyping	17
Questioning - colleagues	13	Structured approach - bail	47

Structured approach - sentence	86
Structured approach - verdict	76
Structured sentencing - youths	172
Summary offences	69
Supervision order	169
Surety	44
Surveillance	170
Suspended sentence	126
Taking notes	3
Team behaviours	15
Terminology	14
Think First programme	113
'TICs'	91
Time limits - bail	49
Totting disqualification	139
Traffic penalties	137
Trial - absent defendant	60
Trial - absent witness	59
Trial - adjournment	59
Trial - sequence	72

Trial readiness certificate	55
TV link - bail	50
Unconditional bail	40
Unpaid work	111
Unrepresented defendants	27
Utility warrants	79
Verdict - reasons	76
Verdict - structured approach	76
Wasted costs	57
Websites	178
Witnesses - bullying	32
Working as a team	12
Youth court	156
Youth - procedure	159
Youth - remand provisions	163
Youth - sentencing options	166
Youth - matrix	174
Youth - structured sentencing	172

NOTES

NOTES

NOTES